DEEPENING LOVE
FOR MARITAL HAPPINESS

Deepening Love
for
Marital Happiness

John C. Schneidervin

NORTHWESTERN PUBLISHING HOUSE
Milwaukee, Wisconsin

Library of Congress Card 91-66834
Northwestern Publishing House
1250 N. 113th St., Milwaukee, Wl 53226-3284
© 1992 by Northwestern Publishing House.
Published 1992
Printed in the United States of America
ISBN 0-8100-0403-8

CONTENTS

PREFACE

The information and encouragement in this book need to be understood in this light: building a mutually pleasing marriage as God planned it is an important part of living your life under Christ. The Holy Spirit begins the discussion of the roles of Christian husbands and wives in Ephesians 5 by saying they are to arrange themselves under or submit to one another "out of reverence for Christ" (Ephesians 5:21). As a fruit of your faith in Christ, then, you will desire to make your marriage all that he says it should be to glorify him.

Since Christian couples want to glorify Christ through their married life, they are looking for biblically sound information to guide them in improving their marriage. They realize that no one knows more about marriage, about husbands and wives, and about what will bring about happiness in marriage than the Lord who has made them and has instituted marriage.

You may already be married, or you may be planning to be married soon. In either case, you are probably looking for scriptural information on marriage, or you would not be reading this book.

The purpose of this book is threefold: to share with you what our Lord has said about the marital relationship; to bring to you the Lord's guidance for working through the chief marital problems; and to unfold for you what our Lord has said about love in marriage.

Let me share this encouragement with you as well: if you and your spouse have had, or are beginning to have, marital problems, in addition to reading this book seek help from a Christian marriage counselor. The sooner you get help, the easier it will be for you to resolve your problems. Too many couples do not seek help until their feelings of love have long evaporated in the heat of their marital confrontations and failures. Clearing up their problems and reawakening feelings of love are then difficult for them.

It is my prayer that this book may serve in the kingdom of our Lord Jesus Christ, the Bridegroom of the church, to assist Christian couples in building a mutually pleasing marriage that honors him. May this book glorify him who alone can enable us to be God-fearing husbands or wives.

ACKNOWLEDGMENTS

With gratitude I acknowledge the counsel and assistance of the following people: Fred Matzke, counselor at Wisconsin Lutheran Child and Family Service, who read the second and third chapters and made helpful suggestions; Professor Wilbert Gawrisch, Wisconsin Lutheran Seminary, who read the eighth chapter and verified the definitions of the various Hebrew words and made other helpful suggestions; Professor David Kuske, Wisconsin Lutheran Seminary, who made a comparative word study of the Greek *koite* in Hebrews 13:4; numerous other seminary professors who answered a variety of questions for me over the years; the entire editorial staff of Northwestern Publishing House, whose interest, encouragement, and assistance made this book possible.

I also thank the couples who worked with me in marital or premarital counseling and those who participated in my marriage seminars. I am indebted to my congregation, Crown Of Life, for letting me work on this project, and especially to the Board of Elders, who first encouraged me to put together the marriage seminars on which this book is based. Thanks also to my wife and children for their support during the months of writing this book.

Above all, thanks be to our Lord — for the guidance, answered prayers, unlimited blessings, and everything that has made this book possible.

ACKNOWLEDGMENTS

PART 1

Deepening Love
for
Marital Happiness

BY ENRICHING YOUR
MARITAL RELATIONSHIP

1.

LEARNING GOD'S DESIGN
OF THE MARITAL RELATIONSHIP

To describe it you need to have seen it. That is true about almost everything from sunsets to marriages.

My family and I are campers. We have camped in every type of weather imaginable. During the thirteen summers we have camped, we have enjoyed many pleasant days, and we have seen many sunsets. Two summers ago we were treated to a breathtaking sunset. After a cool, rainy day the clouds broke up around supper time. A gorgeous, reddish-orange sunburst streamed through the dark, widely dispersed clouds, highlighted by the patches of deep blue sky. That glorious panorama testified to the majesty of our Creator.

I can describe that sunset because I saw it. You can describe sunsets because you have seen them too. But a person born blind cannot describe any sunset.

The same is true of marriage. If couples are to know what a mutually pleasing marriage is like, they must have seen one. But many couples have never seen such a marriage or even heard one described. I came to that realization through counseling couples who were having marital problems.

Since many couples do not know what a marriage is supposed to be like, we will look at marriage as God established it. That description will give you a model for your own present or future marriage. It will also give you a point of reference for the following chapters of this book.

In Genesis (the book of beginnings) and throughout the Scriptures, God teaches us that he made marriage to be a mutually pleasing relationship. The first marriage was perfect and was a model for all following marriages. God indicated that when he said, "For this reason a man will leave his father and mother and be united to his wife, and they will become one flesh" (Genesis 2:24).

A Unique Relationship

God has established many human relationships, but marriage is unlike any other. So let us see what the nature of a marriage is and how a marriage is established.

On the sixth day of creation, after God had made the first man and woman, he established the first marriage. The Lord had formed the man from the dust of the ground, but the first man was all alone. The Lord's creative work was not yet finished. The Lord then said, "It is not good for the man to be alone. I will make a helper suitable for him" (Genesis 2:18). To end man's loneliness the Lord created the woman from his rib. He then brought her to the man to be his wife.

From that first marriage we learn that a marriage is to consist of one man and one woman. While this may seem obvious to us today, this fundamental aspect of marriage has been violated throughout history. Shortly after God established marriage, sinful man corrupted it by practicing polygamy (cf. Genesis 4:19). Polygamy is still practiced in various parts of the world. In the United States it was practiced by the early Mormons.

Homosexual "marriages" have also corrupted the marital relationship God created. For this reason, too, we must emphasize that a marriage is to consist of one man and one woman. A gay or lesbian "marriage" is an unnatural sexual relationship of two depraved people of the same sex. Even the beasts do not have sexual relations with one of their own sex. The Lord says homosexuality and lesbianism are degrading, indecent, perverted acts (Romans 1:26,27).

4

According to Genesis 2:18 above, the woman was created to be suitable to the man. The word "suitable" in the Hebrew means "corresponding to." The Lord made the woman to be the man's counterpart, a human being like the man himself — but different. She was not made inferior to the man, she was made a complement to him. She provided what was lacking in his life — most notably companionship.

From the beginning the Lord made marriage a lifelong relationship. He indicated the permanency of marriage on earth when he said, "For this reason a man will leave his father and mother and be united to his wife" (Genesis 2:24). The Hebrew word for "united" means "to cleave, to adhere, to be glued."[1] When a man and a woman are joined together in marriage, they become like two boards glued together — inseparable. Other passages upholding the permanency of marriage are Malachi 2:13-16; Matthew 19:6,8; Romans 7:2.

The Scriptures reveal that men and women enter the lifelong bonds of marriage by their mutual agreement and marriage vows. When the Lord rebuked the Old Testament Jews for divorcing their wives, he said, "It is because the Lord is acting as the witness between the wife of your youth, because you have broken faith with her, though she is your partner, the wife of your marriage covenant. . . ." (Malachi 2:14). Marriage is a covenant, a binding and solemn agreement between a man and a woman. The marriage of Mary and Joseph is an example of that, for we are told Mary was pledged to be married to Joseph (cf. Matthew 1:18-24).

Marriage is an agreement and vow without any predetermined conditions — stated or implied. The Lord never intended that the man and woman would stay married only if one of them changes for the sake of the other, or only so long as they do not experience marital problems, or only so long as their "love" does not cool off, or only for as long as the husband can provide a certain standard of living, or only for as long as some other condition is met. The man and woman agree to take one another as each one is, for better or for worse — for life.

This, then, is the definition of marriage as God established it: an unconditional pledge and vow made by a man and a woman who are free to do so, to live together as husband and wife for life.

A Committed Relationship

Commitment is an essential element of the marital pledge or vow. According to Webster's dictionary the meaning of "commitment" is "the act of pledging or engaging oneself."

Commitment is a virtue God wanted in every marriage from the beginning. It is essential for building a mutually pleasing marriage. After marrying Adam and Eve, God said the partners were to "cleave" to one another for life (Genesis 2:24 KJV). God intended every husband and wife to be committed to their marriage, to one another, and to fulfilling their marital roles and responsibilities for the benefit of each other.

Throughout the Scriptures, the Lord upholds and encourages marital commitment. Every Bible passage forbidding divorce demands that a husband and a wife remain committed to their marriage and to one another. In addition, when the Lord reveals what the roles and responsibilities of the husband and the wife are and urges them to carry them out, he is advising husbands and wives to be committed to their marriage for the benefit of each other. The Scriptures state that men and women are to have an undivided commitment and devotion to the Lord above all. The Word of God also recognizes, however, the secondary commitment husbands and wives will have under God to one another. 1 Corinthians 7:33,34 states, "A married man is concerned about the affairs of this world — how he can please his wife. . . . a married woman is concerned about the affairs of this world — how she can please her husband."

A Triangular Relationship

God created both the man and the woman in his own image. "So God created man in his own image, in the image of God he created him; male and female he created them" (Genesis 1:27). The books of Ephesians and Colossians define the image of God for us. Ephesians 4:24 tells us to "put on the new self, created to be like God in true righteousness and holiness." So the image of God consisted of true righteousness and holiness. Colossians 3:10 tells us to "put on the new self, which is being renewed in knowledge in the image of its Creator." This passage is speaking to Christians who, by the power of God's word and Spirit, are being renewed in knowledge. That knowledge is in the image of God and is a holy, righteous knowledge of God and his will. When Adam and Eve were created in the image of God, then, they were created righteous and holy, with a perfect knowledge of God's moral law written in their hearts. Even after the fall into sin an imperfect remnant of that knowledge exists in the hearts of men and women everywhere (cf. Romans 2:14,15).

Since Adam and Eve were created in the image of God, the will of each of them at first was in perfect harmony with God's will for their life and marriage. Consequently, the individual wills of Adam and Eve were in perfect harmony. Therefore, there were no conflicts of interest over their marital relationship, the goals for their marriage, or any other goals each of them might have had. Each of them was a separate individual with a separate will and personality, but as a couple their minds and wills were harmoniously united.

A triangular relationship existed in Eden. God, the Creator, was at the top. He was joined to each of them. At the base of the triangle Adam and Eve were joined together under him. In that triangular relationship the husband and wife shared the same God, the same love and rich grace of God, the same religious faith, the same will, and the same spiritual and moral values and standards. That is the type of marital relationship God established — a husband and wife united in, with, and under him.

A Pleasantly Righteous Relationship

When God created man and woman in his own image and with their individual wills united to his, he made them capable of perfect spiritual love. God ordained that men and women were to love him above all and their neighbors as themselves. Their love was to express itself by doing what was right according to the moral law of God as later summarized in the Ten Commandments (cf. Matthew 22:37-39; Romans 13:8-10). Such love was intended to make all human relationships enjoyably pleasant and righteous.

That perfect spiritual love was to permeate marital relationships as well, for a man's or a woman's closest neighbor is his or her spouse. God's will is that a husband and wife also show their love for one another by doing what is right for each other according to the commandments. This would make their relationship wonderfully pleasant.

1 Corinthians 13:4-7 informs us how the true spiritual love of God's people expresses itself in every relationship, including marriage. From the beginning, husbands and wives were to show each other that "love is patient, love is kind. It does not envy, it does not boast, it is not proud. It is not rude, it is not self-seeking, it is not easily angered. . . . Love does not delight in evil but rejoices with the truth. It always protects, always trusts, always hopes, always perseveres." How pleasant and desirable such spiritual love would make every marriage.

Furthermore, since man and woman were originally created in the image of God, God desired the fruits of the Holy Spirit to abound in their individual personalities and in their marriage. Those fruits of the Spirit are "love, joy, peace, patience, kindness, goodness, faithfulness, gentleness and self-control" (Galatians 5:22,23). What a pleasant relationship those spiritual virtues would make for every married couple.

An Adult Relationship

When the Lord married Adam and Eve, he brought together two holy, adult people with perfect personalities. Today psychologists would say each was a mature individual. Neither of them had any sinful traits or habits. Neither of them had a personality marred by jealousy, possessiveness, insecurity, dominance, pride, a lack of self-respect or self-confidence, a bad temper, or other weaknesses due to sin. Being such psychologically adult people, they were capable of carrying on a mutually satisfactory marriage. That was to be the pattern for every marriage to follow. A mature husband and wife are essential to a successful marriage, as we will see in the next chapters.

A Virtuous Head-Helper Relationship

Beginning with the very first man and woman, God ordained that the woman was to be the man's helper. The Lord said, "It is not good for the man to be alone. I will make a helper suitable for him" (Genesis 2:18). The man, on the other hand, was the woman's head.

But what responsibilities did God give each of them in their respective roles as the head or the helper in their marital relationship? That knowledge is critical to a proper understanding of marriage as God established it. Let us first see what the Scriptures say about the responsibilities of the husband, then about the responsibilities of the wife.

God made the husband the head of his wife and the leader in their relationship. Ephesians 5:23 states, "The husband is the head of the wife as Christ is the head of the church." The fact Adam was created first established from the beginning that the man held the position of leadership and authority — even outside of the marital relationship. For 1 Timothy 2:12,13 states, "I do not permit a woman to teach or to have authority over a man; she must be silent. For Adam was formed first, then Eve."

But the headship of the husband was never intended to be a dictatorship. It was intended to be a headship of self-sacrificial love. In Ephesians 5:25 the Lord says, "Husbands, love your wives, just as Christ loved the church and gave himself up for her to make her holy." We know how Christ loved the church and gave himself up for her: he willingly took her sins on himself and laid down his life on the cross to save her from everlasting punishment. Christ's self-sacrificial love for the church is the pattern for the husband's love for his wife. When a husband loves his wife in such a manner, he puts the interests, the needs, and the concerns of his wife above his own (cf. Ephesians 5:21,25).

God intended every husband to be mate-oriented, not self-centered. The husband was to nourish and cherish his wife. He was to love her just as he loved himself. St. Paul reminds us, "In this same way, husbands ought to love their wives as their own bodies. He who loves his wife loves himself. After all, no one ever hated his own body, but he feeds and cares for it, just as Christ does the church. . . . each one of you also must love his wife as he loves himself" (Ephesians 5:28,29,33).

With the position of being the head of the wife and family comes the responsibility of providing leadership in the marriage and home. The Lord has revealed in what areas the husband is to lead his family.

God gave the husband the responsibility for spiritual leadership in the home. Ephesians 6:4 states, "Fathers, do not exasperate your children; instead, bring them up in the training and instruction of the Lord."

Closely associated with the husband's spiritual leadership in the home is the training and disciplining of the children. The husband is to see to it the children are taught right from wrong and God-pleasing moral principles. His wife is his helper in this area, but not his replacement or substitute. Ephesians 6:4 places this responsibility squarely on the husband and father.

God has also given the husband two other specific areas of responsibility. The husband has the primary responsibility to earn a living for his wife and family (cf. Ephesians 5:29; 1 Timothy 5:8), while the wife is instructed to be busy working at home (cf. Titus 2:5). The husband is also responsible for the management of his family and household (1 Timothy 3:12).

Every husband is also to live with his wife in an understanding manner, for the Lord has said, "You husbands likewise, live with your wives in an understanding way, as with a weaker vessel" (1 Peter 3:7 NASB). To do that the husband must consider many things about his wife and about his relationship with her. He is obliged to be considerate of her needs, to bear in mind what kind of woman she is, to understand what kind of personality she has, to consider what kinds of moods she has, and to be mindful she needs his love and affection. He is to take into consideration her health and her physical limitations. He is to treat her as his weaker partner.

The husband is to respect his wife and appreciate her as a precious child of God like himself. He is to recognize that she is under God's grace as much as he is. For the Lord has said, "Husbands . . . be considerate as you live with your wives, and treat them with respect . . . as heirs with you of the gracious gift of life, so that nothing will hinder your prayers" (1 Peter 3:7).

Let us now look at the responsibilities the Lord has given to every wife beginning with Eve. First, the wife is to be submissive to her husband in everything. She is to accept his leadership as the head of the family. The Lord has said, "Wives, submit to your husbands as to the Lord. . . . Now as the church submits to Christ, so also wives should submit to their husbands in everything" (Ephesians 5:22,24). The Greek word for "submit" means basically "to place oneself under," and then "to subject oneself, to obey, to submit to one's control."[2] The wife is to place herself under her husband as the church places itself under Christ.

The Scriptures teach us how the church places itself under Christ. The church recognizes him as her loving head who does what is best for her. The church accepts his word and his will without question and gladly follows it. Where Christ leads, she follows, even though she does not always understand, especially when he leads her through difficult times. She follows because she knows he loves her and will only do what is best for her. In the same way, the Lord intended wives to submit to their husbands, but with one limitation — a wife must not follow her husband if his word contradicts the word of God. Acts 5:29 states, "We must obey God rather than men!"

The wife is also to honor her husband. She is to respect him, not only as one who is in a position of authority over her, but as the man God had made him to be. She is to treat him with respect, for God's will is that "the wife must respect her husband" (Ephesians 5:33).

Every wife is to love her husband unselfishly. She is to be interested in her husband's needs and concerns and to do what is best for him. Such unselfish love is actually God's revealed will for all human relationships, for the Lord has commanded each of us, "Love your neighbor as yourself" (Matthew 19:19).

In the marital relationship the wife is to lavish emotional love on her husband. She is to be his closest and dearest friend and companion. God created the woman for that purpose. In Titus 2:4 God instructs every wife to love her husband in that fashion: "(The older women) can train the younger women to love their husbands." The phrase "love their husbands" in the original Greek could be paraphrased," to love her husband as a friend," or, "to be a friend and companion to her husband."

In paradise Eve was a most beautiful person. Kindness and a gentle and quiet spirit were her outstanding qualities. It is inconceivable that Eve in her state of perfection would have been harsh, argumentative, pushy, or a nag. God's will is that every wife should be such a beautiful person. The Lord has instructed wives "to be kind" (Titus 2:5). He has also taught them, "Your beauty should not come from outward adornment, such as braided hair and the wearing of gold jewelry and fine clothes. Instead, it should be that of your inner self, the unfading beauty of a gentle and quiet spirit, which is of great worth in God's sight. For this is the way the holy women of the past who put their hope in God used to make themselves beautiful" (1 Peter 3:3-5).

A Sharing Relationship

All of the preceding qualities God established for marriage would make it possible for couples to have an open line of communication. Adam and Eve were two perfectly innocent individuals. They had nothing to hide. They felt no shame. Therefore, they had no need to raise barriers to protect themselves from one another. Both could feel free to talk about whatever they were feeling in their hearts or whatever was on their minds, without fear of a less than loving understanding from the other. Being perfect individuals, their communication was not affected by pride, anger, resentment, impatience, malice, mistrust, or other sinful traits.

When the Lord established marriage, he clearly intended husbands and wives to communicate with one another. The Lord gave the gifts of rational thinking and the ability to talk only to the man and woman. Furthermore, communication is a vital part of companionship, and it was for the purpose of providing the man with companionship that the Lord made the woman and instituted marriage.

A Sociable Relationship

When the Lord brought Eve to Adam, he ordained that husband and wife were to be together, for companionship was the primary purpose of marriage. Adam and Eve surely spent some meaningful and enjoyable time together. In the beginning they were alone with one another, and each could discover what a marvelous creation the Lord had made the other. Together they had a whole paradise to explore, a world to populate and to subdue, and a myriad of creatures to rule over.

The joy they felt in being together reflected the joy Adam expressed when he first saw Eve. *"This one, this time,* is bone of my bones and flesh of my flesh" is a literal translation of the Hebrew text. He knew she was the one creature in all the world who was made just to be his companion, and he rejoiced when the Lord brought them together.

Spending time together is an obligation of husbands and wives to each other. We noted before that husbands were to live with their wives in an understanding manner (cf. 1 Peter 3:7). A husband ought to understand, then, that his wife needs him to spend some time with her. On the other hand, we noted that wives were to "love their husbands" (Titus 2:4), which could be paraphrased "to be a friend and companion to her husband." That obviously implies that the wife is to spend some time with her husband as his friend.

A Blessed Relationship

By blessing the model marriage in Eden, the Lord set a

pattern of blessings for all marriages. He blessed marriage primarily with companionship (Genesis 2:18). He blessed marriage with sexual love and intimacy when he said "they will become one flesh" (Genesis 2:24). He blessed marriage with children when he said, "Be fruitful and increase in number" (Genesis 1:28). Companionship, sexual love, and children — what wonderful blessings God has bestowed on marriage.

A Sexual Relationship

The Scriptures make it clear that the Lord established marriage to be a sexual relationship. This will be discussed in detail in chapters 8 and 10.

We have now seen what a mutually pleasing relationship God established marriage to be. He intended every married couple throughout the ages to enjoy such a marriage. Unfortunately, the perfect blessedness of that model marriage was short-lived, and, because of the fall into sin, such blessedness has never been realized again. Now we can only look back to it with longing and strive with God's help to recapture a measure of what once was.

Endnotes

1. Hebrew *dabhaq*; Samuel Prideaux Tregelles, translator of *Gesenius' Hebrew and Chaldee Lexicon to the Old Testament Scriptures*, (Grand Rapids, Michigan; Wm. B. Eerdmans Publishing Company, 1971), p 185.

2. Greek *hupotassetai*; Joseph Henry Thayer, *Greek-English Lexicon of the New Testament*, (Grand Rapids, Michigan; Zondervan Publishing House, 1975), p 645.

2.

IDENTIFYING YOUR TYPE OF MARITAL RELATIONSHIP NOW

What snowflakes are in a snowstorm,
marriages are in the world —
millions in number but no two are alike.

The gentle falling snow blanketing hill and dale and settling on the boughs of the pines is serenely beautiful. The grandeur of that winter scene is so enchanting that we seldom appreciate the wonders of its tiniest components, the little individual snowflakes. They number in the millions, but they are all different in their intricate design.

Like snowflakes, marriages number in the millions, but each one has a complex design of its own. Your marriage is, or will be, unlike any other, with a personality all its own. Marriages, however, like snowflakes, have been classified into various types. Snowflakes have been classified into four types or forms: star, composite, triangular, and tabular. Marriages have been classified into a variety of personality types. These types will be sketched in this chapter, so you may be able to identify your type of marital personality. If you then compare your type of relationship to the mutually pleasing relationship described in the previous chapter, you may be able to see some of the shortcomings of your relationship. In the following chapter we will then consider how you may lessen those shortcomings in order to deepen the love between you and your spouse.

Marriages Are Imperfect

Whatever the nature of our marital relationship, it is less than the perfect marriage the Lord established with Adam and Eve, for we men and women are not perfect as Adam and Eve were.

Through their fall into sin Adam and Eve's perfect bond of love was broken — their love for the Lord and their love for one another. But the Lord's bond of love has never been broken. He has continued to love us sinful men and women. He proved that by giving his one and only Son, Jesus Christ, to save us from hell and to make us his own for eternity. His love for us will move us Christian husbands and wives to strive to conform ourselves and our marriages to his holy revealed will.

The account of the fall into sin is found in Genesis 3. Its details are well known. What we want to note is the corrupting effect it had not only on Adam and Eve but on their descendants as well — us.

When Eve was deceived into believing Satan's lie, she showed she no longer loved and trusted God above all. When Adam ate the fruit without being deceived, he demonstrated he no longer loved and honored God above all. Eve fell into doubting that God was good and had given her all that was best for her. Adam fell into disobeying the word of God that was given to him for his own good. Through their sin they became separated from God, his word, and his will for them.

The nature of both of them became totally corrupt. When God came to them in the garden, they became afraid, ran away, and tried to hide from him. They no longer considered God their friend who loved them. When God gave Adam the opportunity to confess his sin and repent, Adam displayed the spiritual deadness that had overcome him. He blamed Eve for having given him the fruit and God for having given him Eve. A hostile attitude toward God and God's will for him had come into his heart.

When God gave Eve the opportunity to confess her sin and repent, she displayed the spiritual deadness that had also overcome her. She blamed the serpent. Neither Adam nor Eve immediately confessed their sin and repented. Her love had originally been turned outward toward God and her husband. Through the fall it was turned inward upon herself. In addition, the perfect intellects of both of them were ruined by the fall. They both foolishly thought they could run and hide from God, who knows all things and is everywhere present.

Their perfect marriage and bond of love was broken through their fall into sin. Adam evidently was with Eve (cf. Genesis 3:6) while Satan talked to her, but he failed to warn her against the temptation. Thus he neglected to provide the leadership he was responsible for. As soon as Eve had sinned, she stepped out of her role as the submissive wife and asserted herself to tell her husband what he should do — eat the forbidden fruit. Adam demonstrated that they no longer shared the perfect loving, harmonious unity of their wills in their marital relationship when he blamed her for the sin he was guilty of. He had become self-centered and defensive, thinking first of himself rather than of his wife.

Those terrible consequences of the fall into sin have corrupted the nature of every man and woman, making it impossible for that perfect, model marriage ever to be repeated, for all men and women are now conceived and born in sin. All of us must confess, "Surely I was sinful at birth, sinful from the time my mother conceived me" (Psalm 51:5). "I know that nothing good lives in me, that is, in my sinful nature" (Romans 7:18).

In place of the perfect spiritual nature with its fruits of the Spirit, that corrupt, sinful nature produces the poisonous fruits now evident in the lives and personalities of all men and women. The Lord has said about mankind that "every inclination of his heart is evil from childhood" (Genesis 8:21). "For out of the heart come evil thoughts, murder, adultery, sexual immorality, theft, false testimony, slander" (Matthew 15:19). "For the sinful nature desires what is contrary to the Spirit. . . . The acts of the sinful nature are obvious: sexual immorality, impurity and debauchery; idolatry and witchcraft; hatred, discord, jealousy, fits of rage, selfish ambition, dissensions, factions and envy; drunkenness, orgies, and the like" (Galatians 5:17,19-21).

The perfect love and unity of the wills of husband and wife have been destroyed by those sinful fruits of self-interest, strife, jealousy, outbursts of anger, and disputes. What is more, the perfect understanding of God's role for the husband and wife has been lost, and the willingness of both partners to accept and fulfill those roles has been seriously marred. As a result of sin, the relationship between husband and wife has been damaged. Marriages today are not what God established marriage to be.

Factors Determining the Nature of Your Marital Relationship

The nature of your unique interpersonal relationship developed from the outset of your dating to the end of your first years of marriage. For example, when Andy and Susan met, he was a quiet, easygoing person who did not say much. Susan, on the other hand, was talkative and led the conversations. She generally suggested what to do on their dates, and he went along with her ideas. Now Susan is the leader in their marital relationship, and Andy still follows her.

Some of the factors that determine the nature of marital relationships are treated in the following paragraphs.

Personality Traits

From the above example we can see that one determining factor is the personality of each spouse,[1] which is influenced by their sinful nature inherited from Adam and Eve. Whether the man or the woman is submissive or dominant, quiet or outspoken, bad tempered or patient, or whatever, determines the role each partner takes in the marriage and affects the nature of their relationship. Also, what type of person their mate is determines what kind of role each one assumes and affects the nature of their relationship.

Below are some of the personality traits with a few examples from actual cases to show how those traits influence a marital relationship. The names are fictitious.

Insecurity — Tom and Bob were insecure husbands. Tom dominated his wife and home life in order to feel comfortable and secure. Bob, however, was unable to enter into intimate talks with his wife about his life and their marriage.

Jealousy — A jealous, possessive spouse strains the marriage. He demands all of his partner's time and attention. His partner begins to feel smothered. Paul's possessiveness, for example, annoyed his wife intensely.

Self-interest — Vera was so selfish she behaved like a spoiled child, insisting she have what she wanted when she wanted it. She became extremely emotional and angry whenever her personal whims were blocked. In a different case, George was uninterested in what his wife had to say about their life and marriage, because he was interested only in himself.

Confidence or the lack of it — A spouse who lacks self-confidence will have difficulty fulfilling his responsibilities and will frequently depend on his mate to carry them out. Because Bob lacked self-confidence, he was unable to make decisions, carry out his duties, or address his wife about issues in their marriage. Ted, meanwhile, was afraid to tackle household tasks, because he was afraid of failing to do them well enough.

Low self-respect — A wife with low self-respect may feel she is unattractive and undesirable. That feeling moved Liz to try to obtain her husband's attention and compliments through personal achievements, her style of dress, or sexual advances. But Joan felt she did not deserve to be loved by her husband, and she became the object of his abuse.

Natural abilities or inabilities — God-given talents will affect each spouse's ability to live and work at home or at an occupation outside of the home. Talents or the lack of them affect each spouse's likes and dislikes, interests and hobbies, as well as the ability to carry out such routine duties as managing a budget or checkbook and keeping up a home. The strengths and weaknesses of each will directly affect the nature of the couple's relationship. Ed was a loyal, hard-working unskilled laborer, but mentally he was very slow. The burden of managing the family's affairs then fell on his more capable wife.

The ability or inability to show affection — Husbands particularly may be unable to show affection. Such men may have been emotionally deprived by their parents during their childhood, and they may not have witnessed displays of affection in their parents' marriage. The wife of such a husband becomes starved for the affection she needs. She then may push him for that affection, or she may turn to another man to get it.

The ability or the inability to communicate thoughts and feelings effectively — Communication is crucial to the maintenance and advancement of the marital relationship. But the quiet, easygoing spouse may have a problem communicating his thoughts and feelings clearly and completely. Husbands more than wives seem to have trouble in this regard. Because of a lack of communication, misunderstandings develop, and marital issues remain unresolved.

Family Backgrounds

Both the husband's and the wife's family background, upbringing, and life's experiences also influence the nature of a couple's relationship to one another.[2]

The parents' personalities — The personality of each spouse was influenced by the personality of his or her parents. Repeatedly I have seen that a short-tempered, demanding husband had a short-tempered, demanding father, and in some instances even such a grandfather. Husbands who had unemotional fathers or whose parents did not show affection in their marriage were unemotional and did not show affection to their wife either. Ann, for example, had brash parents and was rather brash herself.

The parents' habits — Both partners to some extent reflect the good or bad habits of their parents. Sometimes, however, if a spouse had a parent with a particularly objectionable habit, he may react by leaning to the opposite extreme.

The parents' marriage — The marriage of each partner's parents influences a couple's own marriage. Most of what newlyweds know about marriage, except for what they have learned from premarital counseling, they learned from their parents' marriages. Both spouses bring into their marriage their concept of what their parents' marriage was like. They then proceed to re-enact their parents' marriage to some degree. If the wife's parents yelled and argued frequently, she may yell and argue in her own marriage. But if her husband's parents had a loving, harmonious marriage, that is his concept of what their marriage should be. Mark, for example, had parents who lived separate, disconnected lives. That was his concept of marriage.

Unhappy childhood experiences in the home — Cindy revolted against assuming her family responsibilities as a wife and mother, for her parents had shirked their family responsibilities and had dumped them on her when she was a little girl. I have observed that wives whose husbands abused them had parents who seldom complimented them but often complained about their shortcomings. Those wives felt they did not deserve to be loved and appreciated by their husbands.

Let's Discover the Personality of Your Marital Relationship

Every marriage is unique, but marriages can be classified according to various types of marital personalities. Some marriages have certain patterns of roles between the husbands and wives, while other marriages have other patterns.

Marriage Personalities is a book David Field has written describing these different types of marital relationships. In counseling couples I have observed the same characteristics he has described. Rather than try to "re-invent the wheel," I will draw on his descriptions of them in the following pages, adding some observations of my own, particularly on the influence of self-interest. I might add here that the previously mentioned factors shaping these marital personalities, in addition to religious convictions and education, may be found in his book also. Where direct quotations are made in the following sketches, the appropriate pages are given. Otherwise, to the best of my knowledge, I have used only various terms and facts describing facets of the relationships. I have used the names he used for each marital personality. Instead of referencing every point of each marital personality, let me simply state that my following brief sketches are based on his descriptions found in pages 15-104 of his book.

Let me clarify, first of all, that not every couple's marriage will necessarily have all of the different characteristics found in their type of marital personality. A couple's marriage may exhibit a number of those characteristics but not all of them. Furthermore, some marriages may fit into more than one of these personality types. David Field has stated these same points. What is more, he is probably right when he says some marriages may not fit into any of these personality types, but the majority of marriages will fit into at least one of them.[3]

The Active-Passive Personality

David Field wrote: "This is the most common personality (approximately 28 percent of all marriages). It consists of an aggressive partner (usually the wife), who diligently strives to make the marriage work, and a passive partner, who is led or directed."[4]

My experience has also shown the active partner tends to be the wife. She is herself, an individual. She is reasonably competent and energetic and often has a job outside of the home or is involved with groups and organizations. She has a natural desire to build up her marital relationship and home. She characteristically takes on more responsibilities for the marriage and family. She continues to make more of the decisions. She is the more active parent. She handles the money. She finds the home to live in and the church to attend. She makes the social arrangements. She keeps a full list of things for her husband to do, and she complains and nags her husband for not doing enough well enough. She is talkative and verbally superior to her husband.

The passive husband is generally a steady worker. He is a quiet person, an onlooker. He has difficulty expressing his thoughts and feelings. What he does say may be expressed in short, incomplete sentences. He finds it easier to be indirect in his approach. He may arrange for his wife to find her Christmas present rather than giving it to her personally. He increasingly follows his wife's lead and gives up his authority in making family decisions. He may say nothing about things she has pushed him into and then hold them against her. He says little within the family circle. He retreats from her and his responsibilities as the leader of the family. He retires to the television, some recreational pastime, or a hobby.

Communication is a problem for the active-passive couple. That perpetuates their relationship. They do not spend meaningful time together to talk. When they do converse, they talk about safe, non-threatening subjects like the children, neighbors, work, and the weather. They do not discuss their marriage, its problems, or how to improve it, nor do they reveal to one another their personal hopes, failures, thoughts, or feelings.

This couple shows little or no affection openly through hugs or kisses. They desire them, but such expressions produce tension. They love one another, but they are not lovers. Sexual love is only partially fulfilling, sporadic, and tense. It takes place only when there is some sign between them that it will be all right.

They are dissatisfied to some degree with their marriage. They feel helpless. They lack the knowledge to deal with one another or their marital problems, for they are unable to communicate. They both want a close relationship, but neither of them understands that the other also wants a closer relationship. To make matters worse, neither of them will take a step toward the other and the closeness they desire. Their fear of further hurt thwarts any attempt to improve their relationship and draw closer to the other. It is safer to remain apart. They then continue in a relationship which is much less than the marital relationship God established.

The wife may eventually see her husband's quietness and lack of involvement as desertion. She may feel angry that she has tried so hard but he has not cooperated. She considers him to be undependable, seldom doing what he should. In an extreme case the couple may be so disconnected emotionally that she is numb to the intense resentment deep within her. She may, like one wife I counseled, question why she decided to marry the man in the first place. On the other hand, he sees her as always being on his case. He believes she is never satisfied with him. According to her he never does enough well enough. He is tired of her nagging, complaining, and being overbearing.

Both are frustrated that their marriage is less than the pleasing relationship they wanted when they got married. Being interested primarily in themselves, they both think about what they want from the other and the marriage, instead of what they can give to the other and the marriage. She wants him to be more adequate; he wants her to accept him as he is with all his shortcomings. Their self-interest drives them apart and together with their fears of being hurt prevents them from deepening the love between them — the very thing they desire.

In summary, the active-passive marriage personality may be described as a cold war of silence and unresolved issues. It is an average, lackluster marriage of average people. The husband and wife are two stable people who persevere, hang on, are loyal and dependable and accept the status quo.

The Active-Resistant Personality

David Field described this personality as follows: "(24 percent): Consists of two talented, strong-willed individuals, one who is aggressively seeking closeness in the relationship and the one who is actively resisting the effort."[5]

Both partners of this kind of marriage are often professional people. They may be active in social and civic groups and frequently the leaders and the centers of attention. Both are independent, strong-willed, and have their own views on almost everything. They have accomplished their short-term goals in life. The husband or the wife could be either the active or the resistant partner, but the husband is more frequently the resistant partner, while the wife is usually the active partner.

As the active partner, the wife attempts to deepen the love between them and earnestly desires meaningful communication. She wants her husband to notice and compliment her. She tries to get her husband's attention and affection, but, being overly emotional and sensitive, she frequently resorts to self-pity, grumbling, and angry outbursts to do so.

The resistant husband, meanwhile, views life with a cool objectivity. He is a professional who wants his wife to stay out of business affairs. He may think he is good at everything he tries. David Field points out that such a husband "could be classified as a perfectionist."[6] He considers their marital relationship too close already, so he does not respond by giving his wife the attention and closeness she craves. He appears disinterested. That makes her tense and uneasy, because she does not know where she stands with him. He occupies himself with his work, recreation, friends, organizations, or politics. He shows his wife that he is interested in her by purchasing expensive gifts for her, but she is not content with things — she wants him. But the more she tries to intensify their relationship, the more he resists. He feels her demands for a more intense relationship will smother him. He feels that if he should draw even a little closer to her, she will only increase her demands, and he will never be able to make her happy. He feels he will lose his own identity and his own needs will go unfulfilled in the process. He begins to think he will never satisfy her anyway, so why should he even make the effort?

David Field was correct when he stated their relationship continues as an unbroken cycle.[7] I too have observed that the wife had been pushing for a deeper relationship. But the more she pushed, the more he resisted; the more he resisted, the more she pushed. She was completely confused by him and felt sorry for herself. She felt she was responsible for his disinterest in her, that she was not good enough or attractive enough. She would have to earn his love and attention by being successful in things that interested him. She tried to lure him with attractive new clothes and personal achievements. But when that failed to arouse his attention and he resisted even more, she felt hurt. At times she became extremely emotional, angry, full of self-pity. She withdrew from him for periods of time until she again craved his company and attention. When she tried to grow closer to him again, he felt smothered again. He then resisted as before. So the cycle continued and grew worse.

The behavior of the active wife, whether in the active-passive or active-resistant relationship, is neither surprising nor abnormal. Though her method of trying to deepen the love between herself and her husband may be wrong at times, she is only doing what the Lord said a wife should do in her marriage. In Genesis 3:16 the Lord said to Eve after the fall into sin, "Your *desire* will be for your husband." The Hebrew noun for "desire" means "desire, longing, urge and craving." It comes from a Hebrew verb meaning "to run after, desire, long for."[8] That is what the active wife does. She runs after her husband with a strong longing and craving for him. She very much wants to have a loving relationship with her husband, and she will try very hard to cultivate and maintain it. For that reason the most important thing to most wives is to please their husbands.

Both of these partners feel lonely. They are ignorant of how to deal with one another. They cover up their confusion by acting as though nothing were wrong. Their stubbornness and pride prevent them from addressing their problems. Both feel they are good persons who fail to receive the appreciation they deserve. Both feel angry with the other and at themselves for contributing to their marital problems. Both may feel some personal guilt for their marital problems; but they primarily blame one another. Their relationship then becomes highly reactionary. Each one analyzes what the other says and does, looking for some ulterior motive. Each one then reacts accordingly. They both feel rejected. His resistance makes her feel rejected, while her rejection of his expensive gifts to show he cares makes him feel rejected.

In summary, this relationship can be described as a hot war of two stubborn individuals who both want the last word. It is a quest for a deeper love by the active partner; it is a resisting for self-preservation by the resistant partner. The active partner is assertive, complaining, and demanding; the resistant partner is controlled, reserved, and hardened. They are talented, competent people, but highly self-centered and opinionated.

The Helper-Helpee Personality

David Field wrote: "(8 percent): This relationship is sustained by the fact that one person (the helpee) needs the other (the helper)."[9]

This personality is often a secondary relationship to another type. For example, Ken and Karen had primarily an active-passive relationship, with the active partner being the helper and the passive partner being the helpee. This relationship is oriented around one of the partner's having a problem and the other partner's trying to help him with it. They are often a couple with a marked contrast in background, education, morals and standards, age, vocation, or likes and dislikes.

Inequality is a main feature of this relationship. The one spouse is the helper, rescuer, parent, and project director. The other spouse is the helpee, problem, child, and project. Such inequality prevents a deep feeling of love between them. For how can a "child" feel such married love for a "parent" and "boss"? In its place the helper feels pity for the helpee, and the helpee feels indebted to the helper. They may interpret those feelings as marital love, however, and do feel bound by them.

Because of those feelings, the two do not want to hurt one another by breaking off their relationship. Ironically, the couple perpetuate the problem or may create a new one to maintain their relationship, for without a problem they have no relationship. Improvement is a threat.

The helper perpetuates the nature of their relationship. He does not allow the helpee to grow into an independent person who can handle her own problems. He gives directions and advice. He carries out the responsibilities the helpee should take care of herself. He continues to ask the helpee how she is feeling and doing. To make matters worse, he directs attention to the helpee's weaknesses and failures, thereby undermining any improvement the helpee has made.

The helpee also perpetuates the nature of their relationship. He leans on the helper for guidance and assistance to do what he should do for himself. But at times the helpee resents the help being given, becomes obstinate, and proceeds to do the very things he knows he should not. In that way the helpee shows his independence — but destructively, not constructively. That frustrates and confuses the helper, driving her to a sense of helplessness and despair.

The thoughts and feelings they both have prevent the deep emotions of married love from developing. The helpee feels trapped between the directness of the helper, who treats him like a child and project, and his own dependence on the helper for assistance. The helpee grows tired of being helped; the helper grows tired of helping; both grow tired of dealing with the same issues again and again. The helpee becomes frustrated and angry that the helper does not do a better job of helping. The helper becomes just as frustrated and angry that the helpee does not try harder to change, improve, and resolve his problem. Both feel guilty: the helpee for not doing better, the helper for not doing a better job of helping. They blame one another for the deterioration of their relationship and for the problems that exist between them.

Their problem is they relate to each other according to their own personal needs and self-interests. Though they are not likely to be aware of it, both are interested in trying to satisfy their own needs through the needs of the other, instead of taking responsibility for their own needs and working at those needs themselves. For his own benefit the helpee wants the helper for guidance and assistance to deal with his life's problem(s). Meanwhile, the helper measures her own self-worth on the basis of how well she is able to help someone else. She then helps the helpee to feel good about herself and to build her own self-image. In this way the relationship consists of two takers, instead of two lovers who give for the benefit of the other.

The Macho Personality

David Field wrote: "(12 percent): One partner (almost always the husband) totally dominates this marriage."[10]

The macho husband often has a false understanding from childhood of what God made a man to be. He believes a man does not show his feelings or any sign of weakness, like crying. A man is strong, self-reliant, in charge, determined, insensitive. The macho husband does not consider being sensitive, loving, forgiving, humble, self-sacrificing, visibly emotional — as Jesus was — a part of manhood. He frequently has strong opinions about what the roles of men and women should be, with a limited sphere of activities for each.

The macho husband experienced a childhood of family problems and perhaps an environment where a boy had to fight to survive. His father may have been a strong, dominating person with a bad temper, from whom he learned to flare up in anger. His wife is afraid of him. She would like to grow closer to him, but she never knows when he will fly into another rage. To make his personal problems worse, he may abuse alcohol or drugs. When he is drunk and becomes angry, he may slap his wife or beat her. Not all macho husbands are so verbally and physically abusive, but they do maintain control. The marriage will be run their way. They make sure it is.

The macho husband is an insecure person who has to dominate his wife and home life in order to feel secure. He is afraid of losing control. He is opinionated, insisting he is right, and unwilling to give in.

He is insensitive to the feelings and needs of his wife. Sarcasm infects what he says to his wife, even his compliments, in order to build up his own ego at her expense. When his wife tries to confront him with the hurt she feels, he crushes her with a barrage of ridicule that makes her cry. He is picky and demanding, and he expects his wife to be a "go-fer," who jumps up and goes for whatever he wants.

His wife grew up with a feeling of low self-worth, probably because her parents rode her about her shortcomings. She therefore feels she does not deserve to be loved or appreciated and took a husband who would not treat her with consideration and respect. From childhood she detested conflict. She goes to great lengths to appease, compromise, and do whatever is necessary to keep the peace. That is the approach she takes with her husband as well.

To keep the peace and protect herself, this wife may frequently lie to her husband, as wives have confessed in counseling. She is fearful the truth will trigger another of his tirades. Because she is tense in such an environment, she repeats the very things her husband has previously reprimanded her for. Yet, in spite of the unsatisfactory relationship, she is dependent upon him. What is more, if she is a Christian woman who believes marriage is not to be broken by divorce, she is also committed to maintaining her marriage for that reason.

The husband also has a low self-worth and criticizes the faults of others to draw attention away from himself. He wants people to like him, but, as Field stated, "The only method he knows is to literally *make* them" (his emphasis, not mine).[11] He believes, as a husband told me, if his wife had the choice, she would reject and leave him, "so he keeps her in line."[12]

When it comes to sex, the husband is again insensitive to the needs of his wife. As one wife told me, her duty is to give it to him when he wants it. There is little affection or foreplay and seldom a satisfying release for her.[13] But when the marriage is not so oppressive, wives have informed me they do enjoy their husbands' sexual lovemaking.

In summary, this relationship is one of male dominance and female cooperation. Issues are dealt with by his demanding and her capitulating. The relationship is frequently explosive because of his bad temper. But in some cases the male dominance is less abusive and more subtle.

The Pretense Marriage

David Field: "(3 percent): This is the rarest category. It is a 'make believe' marriage between two people who have no romantic attraction to each other. They have totally different backgrounds, interests, goals, and values."[14]

Field indicates this marriage is most often the result of some external pressure rather than the inner desire of the couple.[15] He notes one or both of the partners may have been rebounding from a previous bad relationship. A widower may marry "because he needs a 'mother' for his children."[16] Young men married to avoid the draft, or the marriage was arranged by the family. Pastors in some church bodies married to have a chance for landing a pastoral position.[17]

This relationship is an empty shell. The couple is emotionally disconnected, and they are not attracted to each other as lovers. Neither affection nor conflict is evident in this marriage as they are in other types of marriages.

What is more, the couple do not talk to one another. They can sit in the same room for hours without speaking to one another.

Both silently wonder how they can attain warm feelings for someone they are not interested in. They feel hopeless and trapped, without a solution to their feeling so disconnected.[18]

The couple have never been committed to their marriage, and because of the lack of feelings between them, they live for other things.[19] Sex is infrequent and mechanical. Extra-marital affairs are not uncommon for either of them. Both partners have their separate groups and activities. Their vocation takes precedence over their marriage.[20]

In summary, the couple is not married emotionally. They are married singles.

Let me share this additional point with you: couples of other types of marriages who are having marital problems also exhibit the emotional disconnectedness of this pretense personality to an extent. The longer their marital problems have existed and the worse their problems are, the more they are emotionally disconnected.

"The Kids" Personality

There is no need for our purpose here to go into this marital relationship of young teenagers other than to recognize it. David Field's description is sufficient. "(5 percent): This is a marriage between two immature 'kids' who are not ready to cope with the pressures of life. They need outside help, often from their parents, in order to survive."[21]

The Active-Active Personality

David Field wrote: "(20 percent): This marriage is founded on a firm commitment to each other, and both partners are equipped and motivated to make the marriage work."[22]

This marriage has noteworthy characteristics of the mutually pleasing marriage God established. The couple enjoy being together. They are committed to each other and to their marriage for life. Both desire to make the marriage the best they can. Their marriage takes precedence over other concerns. They tend to be emotionally mature individuals without personality traits that prevent a meaningful relationship. From seeing their parents' good marriages, they have some concept of what a marriage should be. They are likely to be religious and have accepted themselves as God made them.

These partners cooperate with one another. They make sacrifices for their partner and for their marriage. They are committed to give to the relationship and for the benefit of their mate rather than being intent on taking from the marriage what they want or feel they need for themselves. Through such unselfish giving they both receive in abundance.

Both understand that every marriage has problems. Sometimes one of them will have a bad day, but they accept that and know the situation will soon be better. Furthermore, they have accepted one another for what each one is. In love they bear one another's faults and mistakes. When problems arise between them, they strive to resolve them quickly. They discuss those matters and consider, not only what is in their own best interest, but what is in the best interest of their partner and their marriage. Through such discussions, appropriate apologies, and needed forgiveness they soon become reconciled. Those resolved problems then bind them more closely together than they were before.

Their effective communication enables them to work through their problems and build deeper feelings of love between them. They express their thoughts and feelings, listen to one another, when necessary clarify what was stated, and support one another. Both are free to be themselves. Neither of them needs to be defensive over against the other. They trust one another and know they will both be honest with each other.

In summary, this is not a perfect marriage, but it is a mutually pleasing, loving relationship of two committed partners.

Endnotes

1. David Field, *Marriage Personalities*, (Eugene, Oregon; Harvest House Publishers, 1986), ref. p 27.

2. *Ibid.*, p 27.

3. *Ibid.*, p 28.

4. *Ibid.*, p 26.

5. *Ibid.*, p 26.

6. *Ibid.*, p 50.

7. *Ibid.*, p 51.

8. Hebrew *tshuqothek* and *shuq;* Samuel Prideaux Tregelles, translator of *Gesenius' Hebrew and Chaldee Lexicon to the Old Testament Scriptures,* (Grand Rapids, Michigan; Wm. B. Eerdmans Publishing Company, 1971), ref. p 811.

9. Field: p 26.

10. *Ibid.*, p 26.

11. *Ibid.*, p 74.

12. *Ibid.*, p 74.

13. *Ibid.*, p 74.

14. *Ibid.*, p 26.

15. *Ibid.*, p 83.

16. *Ibid.*, p 83.

17. *Ibid.*, pp 83,84.

18. *Ibid.*, pp 84,85.

19. *Ibid.*, p 85.
20. *Ibid.*, p 84.
21. *Ibid.*, p 26.
22. *Ibid.*, p 26.

3.

IMPROVING YOUR TYPE OF MARITAL RELATIONSHIP

The design of the roof trusses in some churches reveals that the triangle is a figure of strength and beauty. It is a fitting symbol for our almighty, gracious triune God. God also made marriage a triangular relationship of strength and beauty — with himself at the top and the husband and wife joined together under him and united in him. In that triangular relationship the first husband and wife enjoyed perfect love and harmony.

But sin ruined that relationship, and no marriage since has been like the original marriage in Eden. The different marital personalities reveal a variety of ways that blessed marital relationship has been corrupted and twisted out of shape.

The question is: what will make those marriages more like what the Lord designed marriage to be? The answer is: restore the triangular relationship of strength and beauty through Jesus Christ. The marital relationship will be formed according to the Lord's design as the husband and wife grow spiritually in the Lord and out of reverence for him structure their lives and marriage according to his will.

Be Led by the Lord to Improve Your Marital Relationship

The changes in your personality and attitudes needed to deepen the love in your relationship must flow from a penitent heart. Repentance is not just a one-time act. It is a process that continues throughout the Christian's life. Our continuing daily sinning calls for daily contrition and repentance. The faith that looks to Christ alone for forgiveness of all sins is also the faith from which righteous deeds then naturally proceed,.changing one's life and marriage for the better. Such deeds we call fruits of faith. Jesus said, "I am the vine; you are the branches. If a man remains in me and I in him, he will bear much fruit; apart from me you can do nothing (John 15:5)." May the Lord, therefore, lead you to do the following:

Personal Reflection

Examine yourself and the type of a husband or wife you have been. Jesus said,

> Why do you look at the speck of sawdust in your brother's eye and pay no attention to the plank in your own eye? How can you say to your brother, 'Let me take the speck out of your eye,' when all the time there is a plank in your own eye? You hypocrite, first take the plank out of your own eye, and then you will see clearly to remove the speck from your brother's eye (Matthew 7:3-5).

Concentrate on identifying and correcting your own faults before you point to your spouse's faults. By the grace of God changes will then happen.

Comparison

Each of you compare the kind of spouse you have been to the role the Lord gave you as a husband or wife. Note your shortcomings.

Confession

Follow the Lord's instructions first to be reconciled to one another before coming to him (Matthew 5:23,24). When each of you has identified your own failures, confess them to one another. Apologize for them, and forgive one another from the heart (Ephesians 4:32). Then together confess your failures to the Lord in prayer. Ask him to forgive you for failing to be the spouse you should be and for the sinful things you have said or done to your spouse.

Trust

May the Lord give you the faith to believe he has forgiven and continues to forgive those sins because Jesus has paid for them on the cross. "If we confess our sins, he is faithful and just and will forgive us our sins and purify us from all unrighteousness" (1 John 1:9).

Fruits of Faith

May the Lord's forgiveness and salvation through Jesus then give you the desire to be a better spouse than you were in the past. For,

> You were taught, with regard to your former way of life, to put off your old self, which is being corrupted by its deceitful desires; to be made new in the attitude of your minds; and to put on the new self, created to be like God in true righteousness and holiness (Ephesians 4:22-24).

Prayer

Ask the Lord to enable you to correct your faults and to fulfill the role he has given you as a husband or wife. Since fulfilling your marital role is his will for you, be confident he will hear you. "This is the confidence we have in approaching God: that if we ask anything according to his will, he hears us. And if we know that he hears us — whatever we ask — we know that we have what we asked of him" (1 John 5:14,15).

Growth by His Word

Seek the Lord's help and strength through his word, for by his word he gives you spiritual life and faith. "For you have been born again . . . through the living and enduring word of God" (1 Peter 1:23). Then by the Lord's strength pattern yourself after the scriptural role of the husband or wife outlined in the first chapter of this book.

Patience

Astounding results do not often occur overnight. As the fruits on the trees grow gradually, generally the spiritual fruits of faith do too. Because of your sinful nature, you may occasionally slip into your old ways again. May the Lord, therefore, continue to work repentance in your heart, renew you by the word of his gracious forgiveness in Christ, and enable you to struggle against and conquer your weaknesses. As you do, your marital relationship will improve.

Follow the Scriptures to Improve Your Marital Relationship

The Active-Passive Personality

The active wife — If you have identified yourself as the active wife, may the Lord enable you to be a submissive wife. "Now as the church submits to Christ, so also wives should submit to their husbands in everything" (Ephesians 5:24). The Greek word translated "submit" means "to place oneself under, to subject oneself, to obey, to submit to one's control." Your desire for a loving relationship with your husband is not wrong, but your methods for gaining it are if you are pushy, assertive, demanding, nagging, and complaining. To honor your Lord, you will want to place yourself under your husband, not walk all over him.

Be submissive instead of assertive. Back off and relieve the pressure from your husband. The more you demand and nag, the less your husband cares and wants to be involved. Reverse the trend. Quietly strive to make your marriage a relationship he will want to be involved in. Even in winning over an unbelieving husband for Christ, the Lord teaches wives to do it — not by demanding and nagging — but by their Christian behavior without a word (1 Peter 3:1). Remember, too, your demands and dissatisfaction with your husband can be communicated not only by what you say but by certain tones in your voice, facial expressions, or mannerisms as well. Keep them under control too.

Try to see the situation as your husband may see it. How would you feel if you had a boss who never seemed satisfied with what you did? You never did enough well enough. All you heard were more demands and complaints. Would you not give up with a "what's-the-use" attitude, feel like doing even less, and find some way to quietly stay out of his way? Is that how your husband sees his relationship with you?

Replace your complaints with compliments. Try to draw your husband into your marriage and family affairs by complimenting him for what he does. Also ask for his suggestions. A slap on the back accomplishes more than a slap in the face. "Reckless words pierce like a sword, but the tongue of the wise brings healing. . . . Pleasant words are a honeycomb, sweet to the soul and healing to the bones" (Proverbs 12:18; 16:24).

What is more, "Do not let any unwholesome talk come out of your mouths, but only what is helpful for building others up according to their needs, that it may benefit those who listen" (Ephesians 4:29). Your husband needs to become active in your marriage and family affairs. God's word above all can build him up to become an active husband. But in addition to God's word, some sincere compliments and encouragement from you may encourage him to do even more of what he is doing right. The Greek in the above verse states, "If (there is) something good toward building up (such as your compliments and encouragement) for the need," then let that "come out of your mouths." The Lord also uses encouragement to urge us on to new heights of Christian living (cf. Philippians 1:9-11; 2:12; Colossians 2:6,7; 1 Thessalonians 4:1). So give your husband that encouragement. Compliment him for what he does. He may begin to do more.

This is not to say a proper rebuke is never in order or that your compliments are the proper motivation for his becoming an active husband. Compliments are only a human device. The proper motivation for your husband to carry out his God-given responsibilities would be his fear and love of God.

To be a submissive wife, accept your husband for what he is, and submit to him accordingly. Ask yourself, "Have I been accepting the man as God made him and for what he was when I married him?" Reconsider your demands. Are you demanding what he does not have the God-given capability to be, to do, or to give? If your husband lacks the God-given abilities to be the active leader in some aspects of your marriage, serve as his helper in those areas. Let him rely on you to help him with those things. The Lord has made you his helper, but not his overseer to drive him, dominate him, or compete with him for control. Your husband continues to be responsible for the leadership in your marriage. We are merely recognizing his limited God-given abilities in areas you can help with, or making allowance for his need to change until the Lord brings about that change in him.

To deepen the love in your marriage, concentrate on your husband's good points and strengths, not his bad points and weaknesses. Then learn to be content with the man you married, for the Lord has said,

> Finally, brothers, whatever is true, whatever is noble, whatever is right, whatever is pure, whatever is lovely, whatever is admirable — if anything is excellent or praiseworthy — think about such things. . . . I have learned to be content whatever the circumstances" (Philippians 4:8,11).

The passive husband — If you have come to see yourself as a passive husband, may the Lord enable you to become the active head of your marriage and family. "For the husband is the head of the wife as Christ is the head of the church. . . . He must manage his own family well and see that his children obey him with proper respect" (Ephesians 5:23, 1 Timothy 3:4). You are responsible to God for managing the affairs of your household. May the Lord lead you to repent of your passivity and the neglect of your duties as the head of your home.

As a passive husband, you may have limited God-given abilities. You need not be ashamed of that. God made you what you are with the abilities you have. 1 Corinthians 4:7 states, "For who makes you different from anyone else? What do you have that you did not receive?" Therefore, rejoice in the talents the Lord has given to you, and use them to lead your family to glorify him. "Whether you eat or drink or whatever you do, do it all for the glory of God" (1 Corinthians 10:31).

If you are incapable of managing some of the affairs of your household, discuss them with your wife, who is your helper. Enlist her assistance and delegate that responsibility to her. Then stay involved in those matters by discussing them with her occasionally. But don't sit back, relinquish more of your authority and responsibility, and dump everything in her lap. Your wife is your helper, not your replacement or substitute.

Do you find it difficult to talk to your wife about your marital problems in order to be reconciled to her? If so, your problem may be a lack of self-confidence to address her. That is merely a personal weakness, which the Lord could help you overcome through finding your confidence and strength in him, as the apostle Paul did.

To keep Paul from becoming conceited, the Lord allowed him to suffer a "thorn in the flesh." After Paul asked the Lord to remove it, the Lord told him, "My grace is sufficient for you, for my power is made perfect in weakness." "Therefore," Paul informed us, "I will boast all the more gladly about my weaknesses, so that Christ's power may rest on me. That is why, for Christ's sake, I delight in weaknesses. . . . For when I am weak, then I am strong" (2 Corinthians 12:9,10). At another time Paul wrote, "I can do everything through him who gives me strength" (Philippians 4:13).

May the Lord give you such a faith to rely on his power for the strength to do what you need to do, namely, to talk to your wife. Let him be the source of your confidence. Pray that he will give you the courage and ability you need, believing he does hear your prayers. Then, armed with the confidence that the Lord will be with you, speak gently to your wife in a loving Christian manner about the problems you are having in your marriage.

If you lack the self-confidence to address your wife about her dominance and complaints, you may also be afraid to address other issues in your life: repairing your lawn mower, applying for a new job, going to the bank to handle the deposits or withdrawals, etc. If so, first address those issues by relying on the Lord's strength before trying to talk to your wife. Learning from experience that the Lord can help you with those issues may further assure you the Lord can help you talk to your wife about your marital problems.

As a passive husband, you probably have been retreating from your marriage to your television, bowling, model railroad, or something else. If so, you have been using those things for an escape. In the future, may the Lord lead you to start spending time with your wife to work on your marriage instead. For God made marriage a sociable and sharing relationship in which husband and wife spend meaningful time together and communicate with one another. Your retreating to those other activities undermines those two bonds which tie you and your wife together. Our Lord wants you to live with your wife in an understanding manner, realizing she needs and wants you. With the Lord's help, love your wife self-sacrificially. Give up some of those "escapes" to step back into your marriage for her sake. She does not necessarily want all of your time, but she would like some of your time to nourish and cherish her with affection, kindness, gentleness, concern, and understanding.

For both the active wife and the passive husband — Each of you probably wants a deeper, more meaningful relationship, but until now neither of you understood that was the desire of the other. Having that understanding about each other is a good start toward deepening the love between you. But now proceed to overcome the fear of being hurt that has kept you from attempting to improve your relationship. Instead of limiting your conversations to safe subjects that do not reconcile you to one another, initiate some meaningful communication. Admit your fears and ask your spouse about his or her fears. Promise each other you will not knowingly or purposely hurt one another but strive to exercise Christian love in what you say and how you say it. Then start to communicate!

May the Lord also enable each of you to lay aside your own self-interests. If you are the active wife, you probably have been interested in what *you* want from your marriage — an active husband who will fulfill the expectations you had when you married him. If you are the passive husband, you probably have been interested in what *you* want from your marriage — a wife who will take you as you are, including your weaknesses. But may the Lord give each of you a heart that looks out for your mate's interests instead of your own. Then you will improve your relationship and deepen the love between you.

The Active-Resistant Personality

The active wife — If you have identified yourself as the active wife of this marital personality, may the Lord enable you to become a submissive wife also. You also need to reverse the trend of your relationship by backing off. David Field made some good suggestions for a wife to do that.[1] Applying his suggestions to what I have explained above about being a submissive wife, arrange yourself under your resistant husband as follows: Be gone at times when he comes home. Limit your telephone calls to him. Suggest he continue to work if he has to. Occupy yourself with other things when he is home. What is more, ask yourself, "Have I tried to understand that my husband is objective, logical, and unemotional in his approach to life? And have I been willing to accept him as the man he is?"

Why not strive to create an environment in which he can feel comfortable drawing closer to you? Give him a sincere compliment and a sweet, little kiss on the cheek — then leave it at that. If he becomes suspicious, tell him you are not after a thing. Some other time let him know you have expected a lot from him for your own sake. Admit that was selfish. Then explain that you now understand he shows his love for you through gifts and providing a good life for you. Share with him that you will love and appreciate him for what he is and does for you. You will not expect so much from him again. Such an honest confession may calm his fears and in time lead him to show you the real affection and attention you need.[2]

You may believe that your self-worth is measured by your achievements, but that is incorrect. Your personal worth was established when God created you a unique individual and Christ bought you with his blood.[3] Furthermore, the Lord measures your worth by the spiritual condition of your heart (1 Samuel 16:7; 1 Peter 3:3,4). Unlike the people of this world, he does not measure your worth on the basis of external things: how attractive you are, what successes you have achieved, how much money you have, or what kind of home or car you have. But since you too may measure your self-worth on the basis of such external things, you want your husband's compliments to validate that you do have personal merit and value. Therefore, you push him to notice you. If he does not, you do not feel you are a worthwhile person.

May the Lord lead you to believe your personal worth consists of being a wonderfully made, blood-bought child of God, who lives in the fear and love of God by faith. When the Lord gives you that spiritual understanding, your inner need to gain your husband's attention and affection to prove you are a worthwhile person will be relieved. You will have become a spiritually mature woman who have found your self-worth in Christ. You will no longer be dependent upon your husband for that reassurance, and you can stop pressuring him for his attention and compliments.

May the Lord bless you as a Christian wife with a heart that is "self-controlled" (Titus 2:5). The Greek word means "prudent, thoughtful,[4] curbing one's desires and impulses."[5] You need to control yourself and curb your angry, emotional outbursts by which you vent your complaints and self-pity. Such outbursts are the poisoned fruits of your sinful nature (Galatians 5:20). Your husband feels he will be smothered under your demands for closeness and the barrage of your pity-parties and complaints. For that reason he resists you. By the grace of God let your true beauty be a gentle, quiet spirit (1 Peter 3:3,4) your husband will want to draw close to.

The resistant husband — If you have come to see you are a resistant husband, may the Lord give you a heart that loves your wife self-sacrificially instead of resisting her. Ask yourself, "Does my Lord say I am to nourish and cherish my wife, or to resist and ignore her?" If you have feared being smothered by your wife's demands for attention and affection, you have been preoccupied with yourself and what you want. If you would start giving her a little attention in order to satisfy her needs, you could probably begin to silence her unceasing demands. Even a little communication will go a long way.

A husband will praise his wife. In the Song of Solomon the husband says, "How beautiful you are and how pleasing, O love, with your delights!" (Song of Solomon 7:6). May you also learn to compliment your wife sincerely. That is what she wants. What is more, that will not cost you a thing.

Understand this about your wife: to please you is probably the most important thing to her (cf. Genesis 3:16, 1 Corinthians 7:34). That is the reason she tries to win your attention with hairdos, clothes, and personal achievements. She thinks those things are important to you. You may think you show love and affection to your wife by providing for her and giving her expensive gifts. What your wife really hungers for, however, is not material possessions but genuine expressions of love and affection from you.

For the active-resistant couple — You both may need to stop taking sarcastic jabs at one another, which are supposed to appear to others as fun-loving jokes. Does the Lord not say the husband and wife are to honor one another? Those demeaning jabs only stir up hurt and resentment, do they not? Are they fruits of Christian love and of the Spirit?

Both of you may need to realize you can be wrong. You both are possibly strong-willed, opinionated, competent individuals. Therefore, you may have difficulty seeing and admitting your faults and errors.

In addition, you both probably need to stop concentrating on your own self-interests. In the past you both may have been so concerned with yourselves that neither one of you was giving to the marriage for the benefit of the other. If so, is it any wonder you are missing the deep feelings of love between you? Does the Lord not want you to concentrate on fulfilling one another's needs?

The Helper-Helpee Personality

This type of marriage is a secondary personality. If you have observed you are this type of couple, also consult the information pertinent to your other marital personality.

The helper — If you have identified yourself as the helper, may the Lord also enable you to find your self-worth in being a blood-bought child of God through Jesus Christ. The preceding paragraphs on self-worth will be a valuable lesson for you as well, for you are likely to measure your self-worth on the basis of how well you are able to help someone else, particularly your spouse.[6] When you can help your spouse, you feel good about yourself.[7] If you were led by the Lord to see your self-worth rests in being a redeemed child of God through Christ, you would not feel the inner need to prove your worth to yourself by helping your mate. Then you could overcome the compulsion to help him and let him work through his own problems. In that way you would then stop perpetuating the nature of your unhappy relationship.

By the Lord's grace set aside your self-interest, for it seeks to satisfy your own needs by meeting the needs of your mate. Your motivation for helping your mate is self-centered. Through helping you want to feel good about yourself. But true spiritual love, the fruit of the Spirit (Galatians 5:22), gives and does what is best for the other without concern for what personal benefits will be reaped in return. May the Lord bless you with such love. Then you will be able to stop helping your partner in order to feel good about yourself. Then you will be able to do the truly loving thing for your partner — give him the opportunity to grow into a responsible person who is capable of dealing with life and its problems.

In your drive for self-worth you have oriented your life around your partner and his problems. In effect, you have made yourself dependent upon having him with his problems. May the Lord lead you to orient your life around Christ. Depend on him for your true personal worth, inner peace, security, and the happiness you need. He will set you free — free of your self-centered dependence on your mate, free to stop perpetuating your helper-helpee relationship.

When the Lord brings about the above changes in you, you will be able to do two practical things to improve your marriage. First, you will be able to stop treating your partner like a child and start treating him or her as your equal. Such equality will alleviate the trapped feeling your spouse has. You can then love one another as two adults, not as parent and child. Second, the above changes will enable you to stop inquiring about how your partner is feeling and doing and criticizing the slight improvements he does make.

The helpee — If you have identified yourself as the helpee, may the Lord lead you to lay aside your self-interest as well. You are using your partner merely to fulfill your own needs — you want your mate to help you deal with your problems. You are not giving to your marriage; you are intent on taking from your marriage. Therefore, may the Lord also bless you with his gift of spiritual love, which gives for the betterment of your partner and marriage.

Whatever talents you have, you have received them from God (1 Corinthians 4:7), and you are accountable to him for using them properly. Because you know it pleases him, develop and use your God-given abilities in your marriage. That would be good stewardship of your time and talents. For have you not developed the habit of leaning on your spouse to do what you should do for yourself?

The Lord says to be "good stewards of the manifold grace of God" (1 Peter 4:10 NASB). We are to use the gifts we have received to serve others. The "manifold grace" of God means the sum total of all gifts and powers he has given to us. That includes our body, all of its members, and all of our physical and mental capabilities.

What is the power that will motivate you to use your abilities as a good steward? God's undeserved love for you. The Lord Jesus bought you — body and soul and all that you are — with his holy, precious, redeeming blood (1 Peter 1:18,19; 1 Corinthians 6:19,20). You are now his possession (1 Peter 2:9). The Scriptures repeatedly refer to us as bond slaves of Christ. As a "slave" redeemed for eternal life, as a "slave" not by compulsion but in response to God's having loved you and saved you — may you serve him by using whatever natural gifts you have to glorify him (1 Corinthians 10:31).

As a faithful steward, use your abilities for the purposes God has intended. He has given you those abilities to serve not only your spouse and others, but to think and to work through the situations which arise in your life.[8] Therefore, repent of your failure to do so in your married life. Seek God's gracious forgiveness in Christ. Be motivated by his forgiveness to use your time and talents to the glory of God as a contributing partner to your marriage. When the Lord gives you such a change of heart, you will be able to set aside your self-centered dependence on your partner, act constructively for yourself, and stop perpetuating your helper-helpee relationship.

A lack of self-confidence may be a part of your problem. The previous discussion on how to overcome it can benefit you as well, for such a lack of self-confidence may be keeping you from acting independently to handle your own problems. Sometimes resentment over feeling trapped and feeling like one's spouse's child motivates helpee partners to act independently but destructively. Their resentment gives them the independence to do the very opposite of what they know they should do. If such resentment has led you to act destructively in the past, how much more could the Lord's strength lead you to act constructively with confidence in the future.

For the helper and the helpee — You both probably need to accept one another as you are. As a submissive wife, live with your husband as he is. As the loving husband, live in an understanding manner with your wife as she is. May the Lord enable you to fulfill the role each of you has, so you learn to adjust to one another.

The oneness of marriage is not attained through changing the other into an image of oneself. Only the Lord can change your mate through the power of his word. You cannot change him. If you could, you probably would not like him when you were done changing him, because he would no longer be the one you were originally attracted to.

In marriage two separate individuals from different backgrounds are joined together into one flesh. The two do not change one another to be like themselves in order to attain a oneness. They draw each other unchanged to themselves in order to attain a oneness. The man and the woman are vastly different — both with their unique characteristics — and they remain that way when they are one. Oneness is achieved when both accept the other and adapt themselves to the other, rejoicing in what the other is and has come to mean to him or her. Each blends with the other to form a union and body.

Scripture portrays the marital relationship as a head and a body which have been joined into one flesh. In Ephesians 5:23 the husband is compared to Christ; both are a "head." The wife is compared to the church; both are a "body." As Christ and his church have been joined together in a relationship of head and body, so the husband and wife are joined together in a relationship of head and body. In Ephesians 5:28 the Lord instructs husbands to love their wives as their own bodies, informing them that when they love their wives they love themselves. Ephesians 5:29 refers to the wife as the flesh of the husband, which he is to nourish and cherish as Christ does his body, the church. The two have clearly been joined into one.

Now the head is not the body, but different. Nor is the body the head, but different. The head does not tell the body, "You must change and become a head like me." Nor does the body tell the head, "You must become a body like me." Each accepts and is joined to the other as the other one is. As a husband and wife, you need to accept your mate as he or she is, then adapt yourself, or adjust, to him or her.

Let me add this: husbands and wives are the closest of all neighbors. Nowhere does the Bible say to change your neighbor, but the Bible does say to love your neighbor. Instead of trying to change one another, simply love one another.

If the sketch of the macho husband in the previous chapter describes you, may the Lord enable you to begin viewing yourself as an insecure person. The insecure person does not feel safe from danger; he feels unprotected. He can feel more anxiety or uneasiness than what is really warranted.

Insecurity is thought to develop when a person does not feel safe and comfortable in his environment or in the conditions which confront him, particularly during childhood. The anxious person may have been subjected to situations in his relationship with others, usually believed to be his parents, that aroused in him dread and uneasiness.[9] To cope with the uneasiness the child experienced, Harry Stack Sullivan (physician, psychologist, 1892-1949) believed the anxious person learned early in life to engage in "various protective maneuvers."[10] But those "security operations,"[11] as Sullivan referred to them, were likely to distort his relationships with other people afterwards.

While Sullivan's analysis appears to be sound, it fails to take into consideration the controlling influence of the sinful nature. Scripture, I believe, offers a better understanding: the insecure person's sinful nature — thoroughly self-centered, selfish and self-protective — has habitually reacted to uncomfortable situations by trying to create conditions which enable him to feel secure.

For example, because of his sin Adam felt afraid and unsafe when he heard the Lord coming in the garden. To cope with that feeling, he ran and hid among the trees. He tried to protect himself from an unpleasant situation by changing his surroundings. When the Lord confronted him with his sin, which further frightened his guilty conscience with the fear of punishment, he tried to pass his guilt on to Eve and even to the Lord himself. If that had worked, he once again would have been in an environment where he could have felt secure.

Isaiah 57:21 states, " 'There is no peace,' says my God, 'for the wicked.' " The word "peace" in the original Hebrew is shalom. As an adjective it means "whole, entire, secure and tranquil." As a noun it means "wholeness, safety, soundness."[12] Those who continue to be separated from God through sin and unbelief have no sense of peace and tranquility, of security and safety. They are, to use the psychological term, insecure.

Therefore, on the basis of Scripture I believe the basic ingredients of insecurity are sin and/or a lack of faith in our gracious God who forgives us our sin, protects us from evil, and provides us with all we need. Those who are living in sin may feel insecure because of a guilty conscience that fears God's just wrath and punishment. But if a Christian, who knows he has God's peace and salvation through Christ, has learned to feel insecure, it may be because he does not trust that God is with him at all times to help him, protect him, and provide for him in every situation. That is a weakness of faith. The latter may describe you, the macho Christian husband.

The Lord's promises and his gift of faith which trusts those promises can overcome your insecure feelings. He promises to be with you always no matter where you are (Matthew 28:20). He promises to cause all things that arise in your life to work for your good (Romans 8:28). He promises to protect and deliver you from all evil so you need not be afraid (Psalm 91). He promises his strength to meet every situation (Philippians 4:13).

If it is his will, he can miraculously intervene to keep you safe as he did with Peter in prison, Daniel in the lion's den, and the three men in the fiery furnace. By his almighty power he can also work in the hearts and minds of others to direct them to carry out his good and gracious will for you.

This, then, is the Lord's cure for insecurity: "Cast all your anxiety on him because he cares for you" (1 Peter 5:7). By faith take your anxious, uneasy feelings, your fears, and whatever causes them, and throw them onto the strong shoulders of God, because he is concerned about you. If by faith you let the Lord take care of you and your concerns, you will not be insecure. "Trust in the Lord with all your heart and lean not on your own understanding" (Proverbs 3:5). In the future, instead of continuing to feel insecure — pray. "Do not be anxious about anything, but in everything, by prayer and petition, with thanksgiving, present your requests to God" (Philippians 4:6).

If the Lord gives you such a faith to trust him in every situation of your life and marriage, you will no longer feel you must dominate your wife and family to feel secure and comfortable. That faith can change the way you relate to your wife. It can free you from being so demanding, threatening, bossy, and stubborn. Your wife will begin to have room in which to live and breath. You can begin with God's help to fulfill your role of living with your wife in an understanding manner, conscious of her needs and remembering that she is a weaker vessel.

You also may need to change your mind about what the Lord made a man to be. Your concept of a man may be that he does not show his feelings. He is strong, self-reliant, tough, a fighter, in control of his destiny, and the king of his castle. But look at Jesus Christ, the one perfect man. Learn from him what it is to be a man.

Jesus was a loving servant. He came not to be served, but to serve and to give his life as a ransom to save us all from hell (Matthew 20:28). He taught us that he who would be the greatest must be the servant of all, as he himself was (Luke 22:25-27). May he give you such a spirit, so you serve your wife by loving her self-sacrificially as he loved us. For the Lord has said, "Husbands, love your wives, *just as* Christ loved the church and gave himself up for her" (Ephesians 5:25).

Jesus was sensitive to others. He was sensitive to the plight of a poor widow who lost her son and was unable to care for herself; he raised her son back to life for her (Luke 7:11-17). He was sensitive to the need of a bride and groom who had no more wine for their wedding reception; he miraculously made the finest wine for them (John 2:1-11). He was sensitive to the spiritual state of individuals and dealt with them accordingly; to those who were proud and impenitent he preached the law and showed them their sin (Luke 11:37-52; 18:9-14). To those who came to him he showed grace, mercy, forgiveness, and eternal life (Luke 18:15-17; Mark 2:1-5; John 11:1-44). May the Lord give you such sensitivity .

Look at the manliness Jesus exemplified for us in these ways too. He did not demand control of everything that happened to him or around him. He always entrusted himself to the care of his heavenly Father (1 Peter 2:23; Psalms 22, 41, 69; Luke 23:46). Jesus was not a tough guy who fought back and took revenge. When he was insulted and hurt, he made no threats, nor did he retaliate (1 Peter 2:23). When he knew the Pharisees were plotting to kill him, he left (Matthew 12:14,15). He was not afraid to show his emotions. He even wept in public (John 11:35; Matthew 23:37-39).

Having briefly seen what kind of man Jesus was, may the Lord enable you to imitate him. Your gentleness, sensitivity, understanding, and self-sacrificial love will be greatly appreciated by your wife and will deepen your relationship.

You may have some other problems the Lord could help you with too. If you have a problem with alcohol or drug abuse, contact a Christian counselor. If you have been sarcastic and have had a bad temper, you also need to learn how to communicate and control your anger. Those problems will be addressed in later chapters.

The wife of the macho husband — If you have identified yourself as the wife of a macho marriage, may the Lord help you to overcome your lack of self-worth and self-respect. What I explained previously about finding self-worth in being a blood-bought child of God is important for you too.

The nature of your problem, however, is different. While you were a girl, your parents may have directed your attention to all of your shortcomings. If so, you may have learned to think you have little value as a person.

But in Philippians 4:8 our Lord instructs us to focus our thoughts on what is good, right, pure, lovely, admirable, and praiseworthy. I suggest you do that with yourself. As a Christian woman, what good, right, pure, lovely, admirable, and praiseworthy gifts has God given to you that you may concentrate on?

I am not advocating that you become proud and conceited. Rather think of yourself sensibly and realistically.

For the Lord says in Romans 12:3, "Do not think of yourself more highly than you ought;" but then he goes on to say, "Rather think of yourself with sober judgment, in accordance with the measure of faith God has given you." The words "sober judgment" in the Greek mean "to be of sound mind, in one's right mind, reasonable and sensible."[13] You are not to be proud and conceited about yourself, but you may in humility recognize yourself for what God has made you. In the context of that verse he reveals that every Christian has certain gifts which are to be used in the church to serve the Lord, and, according to 1 Peter 4:10, to serve others. Your problem is not that you are proud about your gifts and what they make you; your problem is that you do not think you have gifts that make you a worthwhile person. That is not thinking of yourself sensibly either, nor, as a consequence, are you likely to be using those gifts to serve your Lord in his church or others.

Therefore, analyze yourself and make a list of all the good, right, pure, lovely, admirable, and praiseworthy things God has made you or given you. Make a list of all of the things you do well. That list might include child care, housekeeping, painting, singing, gardening, your vocation, charitable works, works of service for the Lord in his church, or whatever. Include on your list your spiritual values, standards, attitudes, and beliefs that are upheld in Scripture as being praiseworthy. Put on your list whatever gifts of the Spirit mentioned in Galatians 5:22,23 the Lord has given to you, and, if you have one, do not forget to add a gentle and quiet spirit, which makes a woman truly beautiful (1 Peter 3:3-6). In making up your list, you may want to read Proverbs 31:10-31, for that describes the ideal Christian wife. If you find virtues mentioned there that the Lord has blessed you with, include them.

When you have your list completed, read it through slowly. Let it sink in. Begin to appreciate what the Lord has made you and given to you. Then in prayer thank God for each one of the things on your list. Ask him to enable you to develop those gifts to their fullest, so you may use them to his glory in serving him and others. With a thankful and joyous heart cast off that feeling of low self-worth. Do not think of yourself more highly than you should, but think of yourself sensibly and modestly as you may — for what God has made you.

If the Lord grants you that change of heart regarding yourself, you will no longer feel that you do not deserve to be loved and appreciated by your husband. That possibly has been one of your personal problems. It may have contributed to your silently enduring his mistreatment.

When your husband mistreats you, talk to him about his sin. For the Lord has said, "If your brother sins against you, go and show him his fault, just between the two of you" (Matthew 18:15).

The thought of talking to your macho husband about his sins against you may be frightening, for he so easily loses his temper and turns on you. Compromising and appeasing him as you have probably done in the past, however, will never resolve his personal problems or your marital problems. To lead him to repent of his sins for his soul's salvation, to lessen his insensitive domination, to deepen the love in your marriage — you need to talk to him about those sins he has been committing against you. Only through such communication will the problems between you be resolved and the love between you be deepened.

Take the matter of talking to your husband to the Lord in prayer. Ask him to enable you to say in the most loving and effective manner what must be said. Ask him to also give your husband a heart that is willing to listen, to calmly discuss the problems, and to make amends.

When you have prayed, trust the Lord to give you the strength to talk to your husband. Let these passages enable you to arise to the occasion: "I can do everything through him who gives me strength" (Philippians 4:13); "God is our refuge and strength, an ever-present help in trouble" (Psalm 46:1); "In God I trust; I will not be afraid. What can man do to me?" (Psalm 56:11).

To keep the peace and to protect yourself from your husband's horrible wrath, have you resorted to lying when you knew he would not like the truth? If you have been doing that, do you not think your Lord wants you to repent of your sinful lying? He says, "Therefore each of you must put off falsehood and speak truthfully to his neighbor" (Ephesians 4:25). If the Lord leads both of you to make the preceding changes in yourselves, telling the truth will be easier for you. But regardless of that, you should be truthful, for that is the Lord's will for you. What is more, your husband will eventually learn the truth anyway. If he then knows you have lied to him, that will only make matters between you worse. One macho husband I counseled, even when we were making great progress, continued to be perturbed that his wife had been lying to him. Her promise never to lie to him again was absolutely necessary to reunite them. So tell the truth.

The Pretense Personality

If you have this type of marriage, then you know you need to overcome your lack of love for one another. Emotionally you are unattached, you have no feelings for one another.

You could come to love one another in the future. Consider the marriage of Isaac and Rebekah. Their marriage was arranged by their families. When they married, they had no emotional bonds between them, for they did not know one another. Yet the Scriptures state, "Isaac brought her into the tent of his mother Sarah, and he married Rebekah. So she became his wife, and *he loved her;* and Isaac was comforted after his mother's death" (Genesis 24:67). Consider also the marriage of Martin Luther and Katherine von Bora. Like pretense marriages today, their marriage came into being because of external needs and pressures, not because of their emotional desire. Yet they enjoyed an excellent marriage. Luther grew to love "Katie, his rib" very much.

As Christians who trust in the Lord Jesus for your eternal salvation, by faith also trust in his promise that he causes all things to work for your good (Romans 8:28), including what has been until now a pretense marriage. Look with the eyes of faith to see how he has begun to, or will, work your marriage for your good; then rejoice.

To arouse feelings of love in your relationship, perhaps the fact Isaac found comfort in his new wife shows where you, the pretense couple, might begin. Begin with the comfort that out of all the millions of men and women in the world, the Lord gave you that one man or one woman as a blessing for life, someone for each of you to love. That makes each of you very special to one another. Instead of looking at one another with cold disinterest, may the Lord lead you to begin seeing one another as his special blessing. Though now you may not see great reason to rejoice in one another, rejoice by faith in the comforting knowledge that God has given you to each other.

When you have done that, follow God's instruction to focus your thoughts on what is good, right, pure, lovely, admirable, excellent, and praiseworthy about your spouse. Make up a list of all those things. Include your spouse's Christian beliefs, morals, values, and virtues; personality, mannerisms, talents, accomplishments, and appearance; his kindnesses, work, and favors he has done for you. Then take a good, hard look at all the things on that list. With the eyes of faith in the Lord's goodness to you, as well as with your mind, begin to perceive who and what your spouse really is. You may be surprised to learn you have a real gem you have never appreciated before!

As two Christian people, pray for the gift of spiritual love. That love always desires to do what is best for the other person. It is totally unselfish. By the power of that love dedicate yourselves to doing what is right and good for one another. Begin to think of your spouse and what will make him happy, rather than concentrating on what you are not feeling and on what you want from a marriage — any marriage. As you continue to show each other kindnesses, favors, self-sacrifices, and righteous behavior, you may begin to feel a fondness and desire for each other arising in your hearts .

God made marriage to be a sociable and a sharing relationship. May that knowledge lead you to start spending some meaningful time together. In the past you probably separated to go with your own group of friends. You probably have sat in the same room without talking to one another. No love or closeness will ever be cultivated that way. You need to have fun together. You need to do things together. You need to talk to one another. In other words, you need to become friends. What is more, you need to embark upon doing those things with an open mind and heart, trusting that you can enjoy one another and grow to love one another.

As we conclude our study of marriage personalities and what couples can do with God's help to deepen their mutual love, let me say that, in spite of the negative aspects of their relationship, many couples do enjoy a reasonably good marriage. That may be the case with you as well. But let us realize that, if the negative aspects of our marriage were addressed with the help of God, our marriage could be better than it is. Since none of us have a perfect marriage, let us pray, "Help us, Lord, to make our marriage what you intended marriage to be. Amen."

Endnotes

1. David Field, *Marriage Personalities,* (Eugene, Oregon: Harvest House Publishers, 1986), p 56.

2. *Ibid.,* pp 56,57.

3. The Staff of Wisconsin Lutheran Child and Family Service, *Living In Grace,* (Milwaukee, Wisconsin: 10th Anniversary Booklet, 1976), pp 13,14.

4. Greek *sophronas;* F. Wilbur Gingrich, *Shorter Lexicon of the Greek New Testament,* (Chicago and London: The University of Chicago Press, 1973) p 213.

5. Greek *sophronas;* Joseph Henry Thayer, *Greek-English Lexicon of the New Testament,* (Grand Rapids, Michigan: Zondervan Publishing House, 1975) p 613.

6. Field: p 65.

7. *Ibid.,* p 66.

8. The Staff of Wisconsin Lutheran Child and Family Service: p 15.

9. Judith Gallatin, *Abnormal Psychology — Concepts, Issues, Trends,* (New York, New York: Macmillan Publishing Co., Inc., 1982), p 97.

10. *Ibid.,* p 350.

11. *Ibid.*, p 350.

12. Samuel Prideaux Tregelles, translator of *Gesenius' Hebrew and Chaldee Lexicon to the Old Testament Scriptures,* (Grand Rapids, Michigan: Wm. B. Eerdmans Publishing Company, 1971), p 825.

13. Greek *eis to sophronein*; Gingrich: p 213.

PART 2

Deepening Love
for
Marital Happiness

BY WORKING THROUGH
THE CHIEF MARITAL
PROBLEMS

4.

RECOGNIZING AND ADDRESSING THE CHIEF MARITAL PROBLEMS

Have you ever received advice or instruction that was hard to accept? The disciples did. When they heard Jesus say that divorce was not an option except in the case of adultery, they replied, "If this is the situation between a husband and wife, it is better not to marry" (Matthew 19:10). They may have been simple men with little formal education, and they certainly were not trained family counselors by today's standards, but they knew something of importance about marriage. They knew no marriage was without problems. They figured it was better not to marry than be caught in a problem marriage for life.

All marriages have problems at times. The happy marriages are those which work through their problems and succeed in spite of them. The unhappy marriages are those which do not resolve their problems and flounder because of them.

In the second part of this book we will look at the chief marital problems and what guidance the Lord gives us for overcoming them. By working through these chief problems we will deepen the love in our marriage.

Recognizing the Chief Marital Problems

The following are the chief problems I have regularly encountered in counseling troubled marriages. Except for the two at the head of the list, I have not arranged them in any particular order.

The Sinful Nature of Husbands and Wives

The sinful nature must be at the head of the list, for it is the reason husbands and wives are not perfect today. Even couples with good, mutually pleasing marriages must contend with their sinful natures, which lead them to sin against one another in thought, word, or deed. In marital counseling I have had to confront couples with their evil thoughts: hatred, resentment, an unwillingness to forgive, unkind thoughts, disrespect, suspicions, mistrust, lust; and with their evil words and actions: harsh words, hasty remarks, sarcasm, ridicule, verbal and physical abuse, profanity, adultery, disputes, strife, fits of rage, hollering and screaming. All of those sins are the "poison fruits" and "rotten plums" of the sinful nature. It is in fact the underlying cause of all marital problems.

The Self-Interest of Husbands and Wives

Self-interest is a firstfruit of the sinful nature. As soon as Eve had sinned in her heart and had become a sinful individual, she became self-centered. Immediately she became preoccupied with what looked good to her, what appealed to her eyes, and what she desired (Genesis 3:6). The sinful nature is instinctively selfish, self-centered, self-loving.

Self-interest in some form is at the root of so many marital problems. Because of their self-interest, the love of man and wife is no longer turned outward toward each other; their love is turned inward upon themselves. In some ways both spouses are intent on having what they want in their marriage for themselves; they are not concentrating on doing what will make their marriage best for their spouse. Consequently, their marriage deteriorates from a relationship of lovers doing their best for one another to a relationship of takers seeking what they want for themselves from one another. Their relationship deteriorates to living together in a marriage that is much less than the mutually pleasing marriage God intended every couple to enjoy.

Self-interest is also responsible for the breakdown of the roles of husband and wife. I came to that conclusion through trying to figure out what brought about the marital problems of couples I was counseling so that I might advise them what would patch up their marriage. I found that because of their self-interest the partners had been failing to do what they, as a husband and a wife under God, should have been doing for one another.

Here are some brief examples: The active wife ceases to be a submissive wife because she is pushing for a better marriage with her husband, which is what she wants for herself. Her passive husband does not take the lead in the marriage, because he prefers the easier role of retreating and following his wife's lead. He puts her in the position where she must take a more assertive role for the sake of the family and home. The resistant husband ceases to love and cherish his wife, because he fears being swallowed alive by his wife's desire for a closer relationship. He resists for his own self-preservation. The macho husband does not love his wife self-sacrificially, but dominates their relationship to ward off his own feelings of insecurity. In these marriages and others self-interest undermines the perfect roles God established for a mutually pleasing marriage.

Family Backgrounds of Husbands and Wives

Family backgrounds contribute greatly to marital problems. Both partners learned the morals, values, and standards of their parents while they were young. In adulthood they then form their choices and decisions and arrange their marriage and home life accordingly. Furthermore, both partners developed from their parents their concept of what a man or woman is like and how they relate to one another. That concept then shapes them and their relationship with their mate.

Many couples never had a good marriage modeled for them by their parents. Consequently, they have little understanding of what a good marriage is supposed to be like. To make matters worse, they received no premarital counseling to explain to them what a mutually pleasing marriage is like. As a result, they pattern their marriage after the only marriage they have seen close up during their life, that of their parents, bad traits and all.

The high divorce rate in this country is not surprising, nor is it likely to improve significantly in the future. For all of the problem marriages today, all of the single-parent homes created by divorce or unwed motherhood, all of the parents modeling for their children a free-love, live-in life-style — are twisting the marriages of tomorrow by distorting the concepts of love and marriage in the youth of today, the future husbands and wives!

Individual Personality Traits of Husbands and Wives

Chapter 2 provided a sample listing of personality traits that contribute to marital problems.

Communication Breakdown

The next two chapters will address this problem in detail.

Anger and Resentment

This chief problem will be addressed in the seventh chapter.

A Lack of Commitment

The endless lines of couples filing for divorce indicate that a lack of commitment is a problem in many marriages. Commitment is essential to the success of a marriage. More will be said about this in the ninth chapter.

Addressing the First Chief Marital Problem: The Sinful Nature

The sinful nature and its offspring, self-interest, must be addressed if a couple are to resolve their marital problems. To address a couple's marital problems without clarifying for them that the underlying causes are their sinful natures and self-interest and without trying to lead them to repentance — is like treating cancer with a Band-Aid. Unless those underlying diseases are treated, either their problems will continue unabated, or they will resurge at another time in another manner. Only the Lord can lead a couple to deal with their sinful nature and self-interest and thereby lessen these underlying causes of their marital problems.

The sinful nature must be dealt with through daily repentance. In that daily repentance we put off our sinful nature when we are sorry for our sins and by the grace of God believe he forgives us for the sake of Jesus' atoning sacrifice on the cross. Then in joyous thankfulness to God for having forgiven us and saved us from hell through Jesus, the Holy Spirit gives us a new attitude in which we put off our old sinful nature with its evil desires and put on our new spiritual nature with its righteous desires (cf. Ephesians 4:22-24). With such a new spiritual desire to walk with God, we begin to correct the sinful things we have been doing in our life and marriage. We begin to follow the role of husband and wife God laid out for us and do what is right for our spouse. This repentance brings us into a right relationship with God. Furthermore, it restores the triangular relationship God made marriage in the beginning. The additional benefit we then reap from daily repentance is an improving and more pleasant marital relationship.

Putting off our old sinful nature needs to be a daily, ongoing process, for so long as we husbands and wives live on this earth, we will be infected with that sinful nature. It resists and opposes throughout our days the efforts of our new spiritual nature to eliminate the sins in our marriage and life (Galatians 5:16-18). Sometimes, therefore, in our spiritual weakness our sinful nature leads us to slip into some sin against God and our spouse. With penitent hearts we then need to come to God once again seeking his forgiveness in Christ and being willing to amend our ways.

To strengthen our new spiritual nature so it may resist the evil desires of our sinful nature, we need to grow spiritually by the word of God, which brings about spiritual growth. We are told, "For you have been born again. . . . through the living and enduring word of God. . . . Like newborn babies, crave pure spiritual milk, so that by it you may grow up in your salvation" (1 Peter 1:23; 2:2).

"The word of God . . . is at work in you who believe" (1 Thessalonians 2:13). As we grow spiritually by the power of God's word, we will root out more and more of the sins we commit in our marital relationship. The more sins we root out of our marriage, the fewer problems we will have and the more pleasing our marriage will be.

For your spiritual growth through the power of God's word and an improved marital relationship as a consequence of it, let me encourage you to do the following: 1) Go to church each week to hear God's word and be reassured of his love for you. 2) Attend adult Bible classes and your pastor's adult information classes. 3) Participate in your congregation's spiritual renewal program, if it has one. 4) Come to the Lord's Supper often, if you are a communicant member. 5) Read your Bible at home regularly. 6) Have family devotions. 7) Pray for one another as well as for yourself. Ask the Lord to enable you to overcome your personal faults in your life and marital relationship.

As the Lord by his word causes you to grow in faith and Christian living, he will bless you with the fruits of the Spirit: "love, joy, peace, patience, kindness, goodness, faithfulness, gentleness and self-control" (Galatians 5:22,23). Consider how much the fruits of the Spirit will affect and improve every area of your marriage, not to mention the rest of your life.

Consider also that, as the word of God fills you with God's love for you, he will arouse in your heart love for him and others. Scripture states, "We love because he first loved us" (1 John 4:19). The love he awakens in your heart for him and others will show itself through your living according to his commandments (John 14:15). More and more you will be doing what is right in your marriage, and you will be sinning against God and your spouse less and less. That will restore the pleasantly righteous relationship God made marriage in the beginning. Look how this love will lead you and your mate to conduct yourselves in your marriage: "Love is patient, love is kind. It does not envy, it does not boast, it is not proud. It is not rude, it is not self-seeking, it is not easily angered, it keeps no record of wrongs. Love does not delight in evil but rejoices with the truth. It always protects, always trusts, always hopes, always perseveres" (1 Corinthians 13:4-7).

Addressing the Second Chief Marital Problem: Self-Interest

Self-interest, the offspring of the sinful nature, in some way contributes to the weaknesses characteristic of whatever type of marital personality we may have. It affects our attitude. It causes us to be concerned first with what we want in and from our marriage. It then leads us to behave accordingly. When those self-interests are not met, they in turn give rise to frustration, anger, and resentment.

What is more, our self-interests can cause us to be uncompromising and stubborn. If we are selfishly uncompromising in our marriage, communication breaks down. We then fail to resolve our existing problems. Our marital problems therefore linger and mount. Furthermore, self-interests can also keep us from settling disagreements that arise between us in connection with situations, plans, and decisions, for we think those matters should proceed according to our own viewpoint or whims. We can be unwilling to listen with empathy to our partner and to see those matters as he or she sees them.

What does the Lord say about self-interest which undermines our marriage? In James 3:14-16 he says,

> But if you harbor bitter envy and selfish ambition in your hearts, do not boast about it or deny the truth. Such "wisdom" does not come down from heaven but is earthly, unspiritual, of the devil. For where you have envy and selfish ambition, there you find disorder and every evil practice.

This "selfish ambition" is the Greek word *eritheia,* which is also translated as "selfish ambition" in Philippians 2:3 and Galatians 5:20 in the NIV. The NASB translates the word in those passages as "selfishness" and "disputes" respectively. In Romans 2:8 the NIV translates this word as "self-seeking." While the word was used for politicians who tried to gain distinction and public applause to put themselves ahead, *The Theological Dictionary of the New Testament* indicates the word pertained to the attitude of individuals as well, "the attitude of self-seekers, harlots, etc., i.e., those who, demeaning themselves and their cause, are busy and active in their own interests, seeking their own gain and advantage. . . .[1] For this reason, it is best to understand *eritheia* as 'base self-seeking,' or simply as 'baseness', the nature of those who cannot lift their gaze to higher things."[2] In his commentary on this Greek word Lenski wrote, " 'Selfishness' seems to be the best translation of 'self-interest,' which terms bring out the personal motive of the heart."[3]

The above passage states self-interest is actually "earthly." It pertains to the prevalent attitude and pattern of life here on earth. It is "natural" or "unspiritual," meaning it comes from the nature of all people, which is sinful and corrupt. It is "demonic," a trait such as the devil himself has, or which also comes from the devil.

Verse 16 reveals the poisoned fruits of self-interest. Self-interest raises "disorder." In human relationships, such as marriage, it brings about "disturbances, unruliness and unrest,"[4] which are all additional ways of translating the Greek word for "disorder." Furthermore, self-interest raises "every evil practice," or every evil "deed, event, occurrence or undertaking."[5]

On the basis of this verse we can state that self-interest ruins and destroys the peace and harmony, as well as other good and right things that should be evident in a marital relationship.

At this point consider whether self-interest has corrupted the peace and harmony of your marriage. Has it led to evil deeds or incidents in your marriage? Has it contributed to your being an active, or passive, or whatever type of partner you are in your marriage? Has self-interest affected your attitude toward your marriage and your behavior in it? Has self-interest adversely affected the way you have dealt with your partner while addressing situations, plans, or decisions? Has self-interest been responsible for strife and conflict in your marriage?

Obviously our Lord wants us to address our self-interest and selfishness with repentance — a change of mind. Confession of our sinful selfishness to our partner is the first God-pleasing step to take (Matthew 5:23,24). Through that confession we will become reconciled to our partner, who is instructed to forgive us and not to hold it against us in the future. Then the Lord encourages us to confess that sin to him and to find the certainty of his forgiveness in Jesus Christ. Being built up spiritually by the good news of his forgiveness and the power of his word, we can put on a new spirit that will replace our former self-interest.

But what is to replace our self-interest, to improve our marriage, and to make it the peaceful, harmonious, pleasant relationship God intended for us from the beginning? We find the answer in James 3:17: "But the wisdom that comes from heaven is . . . submissive." The Greek word for "submissive" means "being compliant, willing to yield."[6] This willingness to yield to our mate will remove (but never perfectly in this life) the self-interest which makes us concerned about ourselves, what we want from our marriage, and having our own way.

The willingness to yield for the benefit of our partner is Christian love in action. 1 Corinthians 13:5 tells us the spiritual love God desires in us is "not self-seeking." Love is always unselfish. It does not strive after what is for one's own benefit. Philippians 2:3,4 describes how this love acts: "Do nothing out of selfish ambition or vain conceit, but in humility consider others better than yourselves. Each of you should look not only to your own interests, but also to the interests of others."

To eliminate self-interest and selfishness in our marriage, then, the Lord wants us to repent and to put on Christian love. That love notes what is best for our mate and yields for the benefit of our mate. When we display such love, we will be right with God and deepen the love in our marriage.

Endnotes

1. Gerhard Kittel, editor, *Theological Dictionary of the New Testament,* Volume II, (Grand Rapids, Michigan: Wm. B. Eerdmans Publishing Company, 1971), p 660.

2. *Ibid.,* p 661.

3. R. C. H. Lenski, *The Interpretation of The Epistle to the Hebrews and The Epistle of James,* (Minneapolis, Minnesota: Augsburg Publishing House, 1966), p 616.

4. Greek *akatastasia;* F. Wilbur Gingrich, *Shorter Lexicon of the Greek New Testament,* (Chicago and London: The University of Chicago Press, 1973), p 7

5. Greek *pragma;* Ibid., p 181.

6. Greek *eureithes;* James Hope Moulton and George Milligan, *The Vocabulary of the Greek Testament,* Part III, (London, New York, Toronto: Hodder and Stoughton, Limited, 1921), p 263.

5.

OPENING UP THE AIRWAVES
FOR COMMUNICATION

Communication is to marriage what mortar is to a
building;
it holds the whole structure together.

The rope was swung back across the pool to the next
man. The man ahead of me jumped for it as it swung toward him. He caught it in his hands; he started to swing
across the pool; but his hands s-l-i-p-p-e-d down the
heavy rope and — splash! He was unable to overcome
even the first obstacle on the course.

Besides physical conditioning, the objective of the obstacle course is to move from point A to point B as quickly
as possible. But there is a problem: numerous obstacles
must be overcome. When a person cannot overcome one
of the obstacles, his progress comes to a halt.

Communication in marriage has a similar purpose — to
move the husband and the wife mentally from point A to
point B as quickly and as smoothly as possible. But obstacles frequently get in their way. When they are unable to
overcome any one of those obstacles, their communication breaks down. In the communication field those obstacles that block the airwaves are called "interference"
and "jamming."

Too frequently interference and jamming block couples' airwaves of communication. So let us see what will improve your communication.

A Description of Communication

Webster defines communication as "1. the act of imparting, conferring, or delivering, from one to another; as, the communication of knowledge, opinions, or facts. 2. intercourse by words, letters, or messages; interchange of thoughts or opinions, by conference or other means." Communication, then, is an interchange, a sending and receiving, of thoughts and opinions through words and other means.

Communication requires a transmitter and a receiver operating on the same wavelength. As a speaker and listener you must be "in tune" with one another, or you experience "a dialogue of the deaf," "a talking past one another." That is like your television being tuned into channel 5 while the local station is broadcasting on channel 4. The message transmitted is never received.

Communication includes, in addition to the transmittal of the actual words, a number of other signals. First, it includes the speaker's voice inflection and the tone of voice; second, gestures, such as the shaking of a finger; third, facial expressions, such as a smile, a frown, or raised eyebrows; fourth, posture; fifth, other associated activities, such as turning up the volume on the television or slamming a door. Even silence can be a signal. It may indicate anger, resentment, or a desire to punish the other person.

Briefly, then, communication takes place when the husband and the wife are in tune with one another's words and associated signals. When they are not, their communication breaks down.

The Types of Communication in Your Marriage

Sociable Chit-chat

Through this type of communication you and your partner stay in touch with one another's lives. You reconnect your lives after being separated. In the evening you discuss what happened during the day. Another time you may laugh about your husband's slipping into the pond while retrieving his golf ball. At times you talk about the news and the weather or your children and what they are doing. The variety of this type of communication is endless.

Sociable chit-chat is a safe, non-threatening type of communication for both of you, for it does not address the issues and emotions in your marital relationship. Husbands and wives of troubled marriages whose communication has broken down restrict their conversations to this type of non-threatening communication, for they are afraid to discuss the weightier matters of their relationship.

The Communication of Information and Instructions

This is a normal, necessary exchange between two people who regularly associate with one another. The information you exchange may include such things as what errands have to be run, what time supper will be served, how to start the car in the cold of winter. Instructions you give to one another may be concerned about turning out the lights, picking up some celery at the store on the way home, or emptying the vacuum cleaner.

The Discussion of Plans and Decisions

This is a necessary type of communication if two people are to live together. The subjects you discuss may pertain to making your wedding plans if you are engaged, your family budget, vacation plans, how much to give to the Lord, a possible change of employment or residence, or numerous other things.

Personal, Intimate Discussions

This is the most important communication for your marriage. It maintains and builds love and understanding between you. Since this type of communication is usually associated with your individual feelings, it connects the two of you emotionally. You become one. It is the type of conversation most wives wish their husbands would engage in more frequently. Unfortunately, this is the type of communication troubled marriages cease to have, because the couples feel threatened by it. They are afraid to discuss their feelings and the issues of their marriage.

In your intimate conversations you talk about your individual dreams and goals, your problems, frustrations, fears, failures, and faults, your opinions and feelings, your spiritual struggles against sin and personal weaknesses, your faith in Jesus and what he means to you, and your beliefs about various topics based on what the Bible says, your marriage itself, your love, desire, and sex in the marriage. Except for your Christian faith, these intimate conversations are about subjects you would not discuss with others.

Your intimate conversations enable you to know one another as no one else does. All of us erect defensive barriers around our real thoughts and feelings to protect ourselves from the outside world. Frequently that barrier is silence. What other people do not know about our inner thoughts and feelings they cannot criticize or ridicule. But in your intimate conversations each of you tears down your defensive barriers for the other. You come out and express your true thoughts and feelings to your mate, so he can know the real inner person you are as no one else does. Likewise, your partner permits you to know the real inner person he is.

Your intimate communication will be aided or hindered by certain characteristics of your marital relationship and, as we will see, by certain personality traits of you and your partner.

In order to have intimate communication, you and your spouse must be good, close friends. Then you feel you can confide in one another. You do not feel you can talk about personal matters with strangers or your enemies, do you? In your marriage, therefore, if problems begin to linger unresolved, if resentment begins to mount between you, you lose your close friendship. When that happens, you no longer feel you can talk to one another as you once did, and this intimate communication then fades from your relationship.

To be able to communicate intimately, you also must know you can trust one another. In your personal conversations each of you makes yourself vulnerable to the judgment of the other. Therefore, each of you must be able to believe your mate will handle your thoughts and feelings with loving tenderness and understanding; will be a good listener, sympathetic, caring, and supportive; and will not ridicule, criticize, or use the newly revealed information against you in the future. If such mutual trust is lacking, you will have few, if any, intimate conversations.

Overcoming the Obstacles to Marital Communication

From the beginning God made marriage a sharing relationship in which a husband and wife would have an open line of communication. But obstacles can hinder and block your marital communication. What can you do to overcome those obstacles?

The Individual Personality Problems of Either You or Your Mate

A sense of insecurity in either you or your mate can be an obstacle to communication in your marriage, for the insecure partner feels unable to reveal himself in intimate conversations. Such conversations require him to tear down his defensive barriers and make himself vulnerable to his spouse — the very situation that frightens him. If either one of you has this problem, how can you deal with it?

Cultivate a marriage of mutual trust and friendship. If you are the secure, communicative partner, you may then gradually enable your insecure partner to open up. Create a safe atmosphere in which he feels comfortable talking about himself, his thoughts and his emotions. Your patience, understanding, ability to keep what he does say confidential, agreement never to use his intimate revelations against him, uncritical attitude toward him in general — may enable him to enter into intimate conversations.

The information I shared with the macho husband to overcome insecurity may help the insecure partner in your marriage. Trust in the Lord in every situation of his life, specifically in his marital life and communication, may enable him to participate in intimate conversations.

An additional source of help would be Christian counseling.

Lack of self-confidence is another obstacle to marital communication. If you have an active-passive marital personality, the passive partner may lack self-confidence. To open up your lines of communication, he needs to find his strength and confidence in the Lord and to work on building up his self-confidence in every area of his life, as explained in chapter 3. As his self-confidence rises, he may be able to talk about your marriage and to express his feelings and thoughts about it.

Other Obstacles to Communication

Fear — If you are the wife in a macho marriage, you may be afraid to talk to your husband. If the information in chapter 3 helps both of you to overcome your personal problems, this obstacle of fear can be removed.

Fear of only more failures — When repeated attempts to address and resolve your marital problems have ended miserably in anger and arguments, fear of only more failures becomes an obstacle to communication. Couples have admitted to me they stopped trying to communicate and simply hoped their problems would go away by themselves. But if you have had this problem, you know they do not. They linger on and gradually grow worse.

What causes such repeated failures? Individual self-interest: both of you may want your own way, and you cannot agree. Anger: you may not know how to deal with it when it arises. Your method of disagreeing: you may disagree destructively, not constructively. Pride: pride may prevent you from seeing you have been wrong. You do not then admit your faults and make amends. Lack of communication skills: you may not know how to communicate effectively.

Double messages — The sender says one thing but does something else, which confuses the receiving partner. For example, the husband may say he wants to take his wife to her mother's, but he keeps tinkering in the basement. Obviously such mixed signals can be eliminated by the speaker's doing what he says.

Poor personal habits — If either or both of you are impatient, frequently jumping to conclusions and interrupting the other, your airwaves are jammed and blocked by interference. Simple patience and kindness will solve those problems.

Different or Erring Perceptions Block Effective Communication and Cause Misunderstandings

What couple has not had the experience of misunderstanding one another? Misunderstandings result when you and your mate incorrectly perceive the words, motives, or actions of one another. Erring perceptions and the misunderstandings they cause are major blocks to effective communication.

Much of the following information is based on a discussion of human perception in chapters 5 and 6 of *Psychology — An Introduction,* by Jerome Kagan and Ernest Havemann,[1] which I have applied together with my own observations specifically to marital communication.

Human perception is the process by which we become aware of what is, and what is going on, around us. That awareness is obtained by interpreting what we receive through our senses, especially through our hearing and sight.[2]

Our perceptions are usually immediate and without much thought.[3] What is more, they can be in error. They can give us false impressions of other people, particularly their behavior, their intentions, and their statements.[4] Immediate, false perceptions in marital communication can bring about misunderstandings. A great many of our perceptions of other people are wrong. They are nothing more than our own biased, incorrect perceptions.[5] We may then react and respond to those erroneous perceptions — all too often inappropriately.

Distractions — Distractions contribute to our failing to perceive all of our mate's signals while we are communicating with one another. A misunderstanding can then result. Distractions are often caused by a sudden change in sound, an unexpected silence, movements, and contrasts. Have you ever been in a quiet library when someone dropped a book? That sudden noise distracted your attention, did it not? Have you ever been distracted when background noises suddenly stopped?

When you and your spouse converse, each of you must correctly perceive and interpret all of your spouse's signals — gestures, facial expressions, voice inflections, etc. — as well as his actual words, in order to stay in tune with one another. But distractions in your environment keep you from paying attention to your spouse's words and all of those other signals he is sending you. You may then fail to perceive correctly what he is communicating. For example, a sixty-yard touchdown play on television may distract a husband from noticing his wife's facial expression, which indicated her words meant just the opposite of what she actually said. He then misunderstood what she was saying.

Since distractions can cause misunderstandings to arise when you are about to discuss important matters, particularly your marital problems, minimize distractions such as the television, telephone, and the children's interruptions. Then start to talk.

Different perceptions — At times you and your spouse will have different perceptions of the same thing. I realized that when I bought a suit. I thought it was light blue. My wife still says years later it is gray !

You and your mate may understand the meanings of terms and words differently. Each of you tends to concentrate on those outstanding characteristics of words that have been impressed on your mind, and you tend to ignore the other connotations. While you are talking, a certain word may give rise to a different perception in each of your minds, resulting in a misunderstanding.

Let me illustrate that with a very basic word everyone uses — "love." I have learned from questionnaires couples have filled out for me that the word "love" may mean any of the following: to give, to be fond of, sexual desire, romance, to belong to, infatuation, companionship, sharing, the most important one in my life. So when you say to your spouse, "I love you," what do you mean, and what does your spouse understand?

During the marriage seminars I have conducted, I had

all of the husbands and wives write their definition of love on a sheet of paper without their spouses seeing it. Then I had the couples compare their definitions. Not one husband and wife had the same definition! So if the two of you can have different perceptions of what such a basic word as "love" means, of how many other words do you have different perceptions? Do you see how the two of you can have misunderstandings because of your different perceptions of words?

Words frequently have more than one meaning. When you are talking to one another, you may understand one meaning of a certain word while your spouse may understand another. A misunderstanding results. For example, a recruit on furlough may mention "his outfit" to his wife. He meant his battalion. She thought of his uniform.

A great many words stand for some concept of a common characteristic or of a relationship among various objects or events.[6] When you use one of those words, you may perceive one thing and your spouse another. For example, in one of your conversations your spouse may use the word "vehicle." You then think of an automobile, while your spouse was thinking of a pick-up truck. You misunderstood one another.

Your perceptions are influenced by a variety of factors[7] — Kagan and Havemann stated, "In everyday terminology, our perceptual expectations are dependent on our state of mind, and our state of mind, in turn, depends upon the situation of the moment and upon all kinds of prior experience and learning."[8] I will apply their observations to the relationship of a husband and wife and to their communication.

Your perception of your mate at any given time will depend on what you have learned about him in the past.[9] If you as a wife know, for example, that your husband dislikes a relative, you may perceive his going out for cigarettes as a way to avoid that visiting relative. But is that really the truth?

Your perceptions of your mate will also be colored by your own physical, mental, and emotional state at the time.[10] You probably have noticed that being tired or irritable affects how you see your mate and react to his words. Depending upon your mental or emotional state, you will perceive only some of your mate's words and associated signals; others you will not notice. You may notice several of his frowns, but you may not notice his smiles in between, and so you imagine your spouse is upset with you.

Your expectations will also influence your perceptions. "All other things being equal, we tend to perceive what we expect to perceive."[11] If your husband has lied to you in the past, you will tend to expect more lies, and you will perceive his words and actions accordingly. You will be suspicious and have trouble believing what he tells you.

Your biological drives, motives, interests, and values also influence your perceptions in your marriage.[12] A husband who has a strong sexual drive, for example, may tend to perceive during the evening those things which he believes communicate his wife's desire for him.

Your motives influence your perceptions. We regularly see that in the conversation and behavior of the wife, for example. A wife is highly motivated to please her husband, and she tends to operate from that motivational, and emotional, level. Consequently, a wife will frequently perceive her husband's words and actions in terms of approval or disapproval.

How many times, for instance, if you are the husband, have you asked your wife a simple, factual question, but you received the highly emotional response, "Why? Don't you like it?" All you asked was where she bought the roast for supper or the dress she is wearing, right? But that she did not say, did she? Your wife had a reason for responding as she did. She was more concerned about having your approval than about where she got the roast or bought the dress. She perceived in your questions that you might not be pleased with what she had done and, consequently, that you were less than fully pleased with her. She therefore responded from the standpoint of approval or disapproval rather than from the standpoint of what were the basic facts, which were all you had asked for. What was the result of her unwarranted perception? A misunderstanding. Her perception caused her to be out of tune with what you asked.

Your emotions affect your perceptions. In counseling married couples I have observed that the emotion of resentment due to unresolved problems especially influences the perceptions of couples. Let's say you are a resentful wife. As you are cooking supper, your husband gives you a kiss on the back of your neck. Being resentful of the past problems between you, which have not been cleared up, you perceive his kiss as one more of his attempts to go on with your marriage as though nothing were wrong. But actually he was beginning to try to tell you he was sorry for what had happened and that he loved you. As a resentful wife, you perceived what you wanted or expected to perceive, which is typical in troubled marriages even during the reconciliation process. In this case your erring perception caused you to miss out on an opportunity for reconciliation.

Your personal self-interests will also affect your perceptions. If you are a self-centered husband, for example, your selfishness may sometimes lead you to falsely interpret your wife's words. Let's say you were planning to go fishing last Saturday. On Friday your wife asked you to go shopping the next day to buy the children new shoes for school. Being intent on having your own way, you perceived your wife was trying to keep you from going fishing. Actually, the children did need new shoes for school on Monday, but you blamed your wife for trying to ruin your fishing trip, which she in fact never intended to do.

Clarifying False Perceptions to Avoid Misunderstandings

Since erring and different perceptions arise in marriages, you need to prevent those perceptions from causing misunderstandings.

Feed back and clarify — Feed back to your spouse what you perceived and thought he communicated to you. Then let him clarify for you what he really meant. For example, if you are the wife whose husband asks you where you got the roast or bought the dress, instead of thinking he may not be pleased with you, ask him, "Do you only want to know where I got it? Or are you saying you do not like it?" Then he can clarify for you what was on his mind, and a misunderstanding can be prevented.

When you feed back and clarify what was said, you are following our Lord's instructions. He says, "Let everyone be quick to hear, slow to speak, and slow to anger" (James 1:19 NASB). When you feed back what you perceived your spouse to say and ask him to clarify what he meant, you are indicating you want to hear more so you do not misunderstand him. You are being "quick to hear." When you then wait for his clarification before jumping to the wrong conclusion and saying what would be inappropriate, you are being "slow to speak." Through this process your communication can proceed smoothly and effectively.

Overcoming a Total Breakdown in Communication: The Marital Conference Table

Frequently couples who are having serious marital problems are no longer able to talk to one another. Their previous attempts to discuss their problems ended in arguments and anger fifty percent of the time or more. Therefore they were unable to resolve their problems.

If you have had a similar breakdown of communication in your marriage, the marital conference table may help you, as it has helped others I have counseled.

Both of you agree to hold a daily conference to restore communication and to continue doing this as long as such conferences are needed.

You agree to meet at a regular time each day, when you can meet in private without the children's interruptions or other distractions. It may be advisable to pick a place in your home that is a neutral spot, not the scene of your previous arguments.

Both of you agree not to discuss any problems that may arise during the day until you hold your conference that evening. Bickering during the day is not going to resolve anything. But let me add, you should resolve those matters before day's end (cf. Ephesians 4:26).

Begin your conferences by reading Ephesians 4:17-32 aloud. There the Lord instructs you how to talk to one another and to treat one another and to put off your sinful ways of the past.

Then pray together. Ask the Lord, by the power of that Scripture reading and his Spirit, to bless each of you with the fruits of the Spirit mentioned earlier. Pray, believing he will answer your prayer. Such a prayer is according to his will (cf. 1 John 5:14,15).

At the beginning of each conference, agree to attack your problems, not one another. This will be discussed in the next chapter. Agree also to resolve your anger as soon as it starts to arise. This will be discussed in the chapter on anger.

Agree on some type of silent signal you may give to one another. The signal may be a raised hand or finger, for example. The signal indicates that, in your opinion, your partner has stopped communicating and retreated into silence or arguing, or the signal indicates that you have begun to feel provoked and angry. Upon seeing the signal, your partner agrees to stop arguing or to start talking again. If the signal indicates the signaling partner is beginning to feel angry, he then explains what was making him feel angry, and you begin the process of feedback and clarification explained above. When the cause of the anger has been uncovered and resolved, you can proceed with the discussion of your problem.

Agree that you will try to eliminate your bad habits that block communication: impatience, jumping to conclusions, and interrupting.

Begin every conference by confessing your faults to each other and asking your mate to forgive you for the problems you have caused in your marriage. That follows the Lord's instructions in Matthew 5:23-25 to settle the problems you are responsible for before going to the Lord to be reconciled to him.

After your spouse has confessed his faults to you, forgive him as the Lord tells you to do in Ephesians 4:32. Remember, you are to forgive your spouse as your heavenly Father forgives you. If you do not forgive your spouse his sins against you, your Father will not forgive you your sins against him (cf. Matthew 6:14,15). Using the exact words, "I forgive you," is best. Other expressions like, "Forget it," or, "Oh, that's all right," only shrug the issue off. They do not communicate the fact you are really forgiving your mate. Such sincere forgiveness removes resentment toward each other from your hearts — a resentment that drives out the feelings of love which had bound you together.

Each of you should then ask your partner to help you overcome your faults by giving you small, loving reminders when you start slipping into your bad habits again. Such helpful reminders are in the spirit of Matthew 18:15: "If your brother sins against you, go and show him his fault, just between the two of you." Those helpful reminders show one another your sins as they are reoccurring and help nip them in the bud.

Praying together, take your individual faults to God, in order to be reconciled to him. Take turns confessing your faults to the Lord and asking him for his forgiveness. Express to him your desire as a penitent sinner to overcome your faults. Ask the Lord by the power of his word and Spirit to enable you to change and behave differently in your marriage and toward your spouse. Then read 1 John 1:5-2:6 and 5:14,15 to strengthen your faith in the Lord's forgiveness and assistance.

Having done all of the above, discuss other marital problems or any faults of your partner which he did not confess by himself. As you talk about your partner's faults, let each of you do it in the spirit of Galatians 6:1 and 1 Corinthians 13:4-7, gently, showing Christian love in saying what must be said in the kindest possible way.

At your first conference I suggest the two of you set up an agenda of all the marital problems you must discuss and resolve. Put what both of you believe are the easiest problems to discuss at the top of your list and the hardest problems at the bottom. Resolve the first problem on your list before proceeding to the second; the second before taking up the third, and so on. Solving the easiest problems first can give you the needed experience and confidence to tackle the knottier problems later.

Any problems concerning your sexual relationship would best be put at the very bottom of your list and saved for last, for a breakdown in your sexual relationship is probably the result of the other problems in your marriage. As you clear up the other problems and resentments in your marriage, your sexual relationship is likely to improve at the same time.

Daily devotions, Bible reading, and regular hearing of God's word in church are so necessary to strengthen you spiritually for carrying out the resolutions you make in your conferences. It is through the power of his word that the Holy Spirit answers your prayers for his help. Therefore, make the word of God a regular part of your life.

Common-Sense, Courteous Tips for Improving Your Communication

Poor communication habits are obstacles to effective communication. Therefore, let us look at some pointers on how to be a good listener and speaker.

Tips for Being a Good Listener

Stop whatever you are doing to give your full attention to your spouse when he talks to you. If you cannot give him your full attention just then, arrange a time to talk to him later. That is better than pretending to listen while you are actually ignoring him.

Look at your mate while he is talking to you to reassure him you are paying attention.

Observe all the signals your partner is communicating to you, such as his gestures and facial expressions, for they shade and may change the meaning of his words.

Listen with empathy to your partner. In love look unselfishly at his concerns and interests to see them as he does.

Feed back what you understood your spouse to mean, when you think that is necessary. Let him clarify for you what he meant in order to avoid a misunderstanding.

Don't interrupt your partner. Your interruptions prevent him from explaining his viewpoint, so that you may see the situation as he does. All too often your interruptions may prolong your misunderstandings. You are so busy expressing your own thoughts that you miss the vital information your spouse is trying to give you, information that might be able to clear up the whole discussion and settle the matter.

Don't jump to conclusions while your mate is talking, as though you know what he is going to say before he says it. More often than not, you will jump to something your mate never intended to say. Only the Lord is omniscient. Regarding the person who jumps to conclusions and interrupts, the Lord says: "He who answers before listening — that is his folly and his shame" (Proverbs 18:13).

Ask your spouse to clarify how he sees the object or issue you are talking about. His perception could be completely different from yours.

Take into consideration the mood and the emotions of your spouse. React first to his emotional state, then to the facts. Don't respond to your wife's frustrations from taking care of the children all day by giving her a lecture on child care. She simply wants understanding and support, not factual instructions. What is more, don't overreact to a mere ventilation of your spouse's frustration over something that has nothing to do with you. In those instances the best course of action is to say nothing and to let it pass as an emotional outlet. Furthermore, interpret his words in the light of his emotional or physical state, such as anger, irritability, weariness. At those times people may say things they do not mean or that they later regret.

Be honest and tell your spouse when your attention was distracted or your mind wandered from what he was saying. Apologize and ask him to repeat what he said.

Ask your mate to clarify what he means when you are receiving a double message. If he says he wants to take you out to dinner, but he keeps sitting on the couch, ask him, "Then why do you keep sitting on the couch? Don't you feel good?"

Tips for Being a Good Speaker

Avoid direct confrontations and conflicts by speaking in the first person "I" instead of the second person "you."

When you talk about your marital problems or your mate's faults using the second person "you," you assume a judgmental attitude that accuses him of being the one to blame. The sinful nature of your spouse, like your own, is proud. It will quickly take the defensive to justify his words and actions against what he sees as an attack from you. An argument will then result.

A more effective approach is to speak about yourself, how you feel because of the problem he is causing, and how you are affected by it. Then enlist his help in dealing with the issue and resolving it. You are more likely to get a good hearing and his support in that way than by accusing him and raising his defenses. For

Soothing is the mate who says, "I . . . I . . . ;"
But irritating is the spouse who asserts, "You! . . . You!"

Your saying, "I feel left out of your life when I cannot share your problems and support you in them," is more likely to get good results than if you said, "You don't ever talk to me about what is on your mind! Why don't you ever tell me about your problems?" Remember, a glancing sideswipe is not nearly as disastrous as a head-on collision!

Save those direct approaches in the second person "you" for genuine, personal compliments. "You look beautiful this evening." "What a handy man you are!"

If you have trouble putting your thoughts and feelings into words, take the time to think through what it is you want to say and what words you want to use. Then proceed slowly and deliberately to say them in complete sentences, not just in phrases of two or four words. You need to express what is on your mind in clear, complete thoughts, so your mate can understand you correctly. This may be difficult for you at first, but with practice it should become easier.

Choose words and terms your spouse understands in the same sense you do. When necessary, take the time to define what you mean with the word you are using .

When you have said what you meant to say, clarify what you said. Make sure your spouse understood it clearly and that you stated it properly. Expressing the same thought again in different words is helpful to your spouse. Rephrasing eliminates misunderstandings.

Express your thoughts in logical steps that lead to your conclusion. A logical presentation is especially important during a disagreement. Proceed logically from point A to point B to point C, and then to your final conclusion D. Don't skip points B and C and jump from A to D. You cannot expect your mate to make that mental jump and understand what logical steps you went through to reach your conclusion. You have to lead him, point by point, to your conclusion. Then, if your mate still does not agree with you, at least he has been taken step-by-step through your thinking process. He understands where you are coming from and how you got to where you are. He can then show you your mistakes as he sees them and explain where and why he differs with you. The two of you will have pinpointed how you have come to two different conclusions. Then you can work toward a mutual understanding and agreement.

Let me show you an example of expressing your thoughts in logical steps that lead to your conclusion and what happens when you do not. Let's say you and your spouse did not agree on what new sectional sofa to purchase for your home.

You say, "I want to purchase the sectional we saw at Rickety Furniture Sales. We can save $150 by buying that one."

Your spouse responds:

> *Point A.* "I do not agree."
>
> *Point B.* "That sectional is not as sturdy as the one we saw at Weechargmore Furniture Store. The one at Weechargmore will stand up over the years better than the one at Rickety Furniture."
>
> *Point C.* "Also, I measured our living room wall and both sectionals. The sectional at Rickety Furniture is eight inches too long. It won't fit into the space we have. The sectional at Weechargmore will fit perfectly."
>
> *Point D.* "We should buy the sectional at Weechargmore, even if it costs $150 more."

Now what would have happened if your mate had skipped from point A to point D when he was talking? An argument? Most likely. The skipping of points B and C would have left you in the dark. You would not have been able to understand how your partner could jump to the conclusion that it would be better to buy the more expensive sectional. But if he expressed all of his points in that logical, step-by-step presentation, you would have been able to follow him and agree with his conclusion. The disagreement would have come to an end right then and there.

When there has been a sudden distraction, assume your mate's attention was distracted from what you were saying. Repeat your words and then proceed.

Clarify your perception of the object or issue at hand. Let your spouse see it as you do. His perception of it may be different from yours. You may be able to put an end to a misunderstanding even before it begins.

If you want your mate to know you have changed for the better, say so. Otherwise your spouse is likely to interpret what you are saying on the basis of what he knows about you in the past. You want your partner to know he or she can understand you as you are at the moment, not as you were previously. But remember that you are going to have to show your mate you have changed by what you do and say from then on. Your actions will speak louder than your words.

The Lord's Word for Improving Your Marital Communication

Tell the truth at all times. Don't ever lie to your spouse. Otherwise your spouse will not trust you even when you are telling the truth. What is more, your lies are a sin against God. The Lord says, "Each of you must put off falsehood and speak truthfully to his neighbor" (Ephesians 4:25).

Marital problems and personal hurts must be discussed truthfully in order to end them. The spouse who says everything is all right, when in fact he is feeling bitterness, hurt, dislike, is a liar. The Lord says, "He who conceals his hatred has lying lips" (Proverbs 10:18). Those undiscussed and unresolved matters have a nasty way of piling up. Remember the old adage: "You can sweep only so much dirt under the rug before you start to trip over it." You must resolve little problems as they arise, or they will develop into serious trouble over a period of time.

Communicate to build up your partner, not to tear him down. "Do not let any unwholesome talk come out of your mouths, but only what is helpful for building others up according to their needs, that it may benefit those who listen" (Ephesians 4:29). The purpose of your talking to your partner should be to impart some thought or knowledge that will bless him. Therefore, when you talk about your partner's faults, say what he needs to hear to build him up in that area of his life. Be ready to show him from the word of God what his problem is and what the Lord says he needs to do. Also, when you dislike how your partner has been doing something, before you talk to him about it, be ready to explain to him how he could do it better.

Don't resort to filthy name-calling and foul language. The preceding passage says you are not to let any unwholesome words come out of your mouth. The word "unwholesome" in the Greek primarily means "rotten."[13] Out of love for your Lord and your spouse you will want to avoid peppering your language with rotten words.

Attack your problem, not your partner. Point out your partner's faults in the kindest manner possible. You are more likely to have him listen favorably if you do. Look at what the Scriptures say: "Pleasant words are a honeycomb, sweet to the soul and healing to the bones" (Proverbs 16:24). "A gentle answer turns away wrath, but a harsh word stirs up anger" (Proverbs 15:1). "The tongue that brings healing is a tree of life, but a deceitful tongue crushes the spirit" (Proverbs 15:4).

Love — to communicate better. If the works of love in 1 Corinthians 13:4-7 were applied to your communicating, they would keep the airwaves between you open. The next chapter will apply those works of love to dealing with disagreements and curbing conflicts.

Endnotes

1. Jerome Kagan and Ernest Havemann, *Psychology — An Introduction,* (New York, Chicago, San Francisco, Atlanta: Harcourt, Brace & World, Inc., 1968).

2. *Ibid.,* p 154.

3. *Ibid.,* pp 154, 155.

4. *Ibid.,* pp 154, 155.

5. *Ibid.,* p 155.

6. *Ibid.,* p 199.

7. *Ibid.,* pp 190-193.

8. *Ibid.,* p 192.

9. *Ibid.,* pp 190,191.

10. *Ibid.,* pp 163,191.

11. *Ibid.,* p 190.

12. *Ibid.,* p 193.

13. Greek *sapros;* F. Wilbur Gingrich, *Shorter Lexicon of the Greek New Testament,* (Chicago and London: The University of Chicago Press, 1973) p 195.

6.

DEALING WITH DISAGREEMENTS AND CURBING CONFLICTS

Couples who attack their problems stay together;
But spouses who assault one another drift apart.

How many disagreements, often over the dumbest things like how to hang a roll of toilet paper, turn into full-scale arguments during the course of a couple's marriage? How many times has it happened in your marriage?

In the beginning, the first marriage was not plagued with disagreements and conflicts. It enjoyed perfect harmony of the wills. But after sin had corrupted man and woman, disagreements and conflicts arose. They have been in marriages ever since. Let us, then, observe this truth: the couple who learn how to settle their disagreements and to curb their conflicts are the couple who have a lasting, happy, *generally* harmonious marriage.

I emphasized the word "generally" because every couple have disagreements during their marriage, including some conflicts serious enough to cause them to raise their voices to one another. You undoubtedly have had such conflicts too, or if you are engaged, you will when you are married, for you both have your sinful natures which too quickly stir up strife.

Therefore, do not expect the guidance you will find in this chapter to forever eliminate disagreements and conflicts. Only in heaven will you enjoy such bliss. Here on earth your Christian life is a process of conforming more and more to the will of God, as you will be perfectly conformed in heaven. Hopefully, by the grace of God, this chapter will aid and guide you in that spiritual growth. To that end let us look at what you, under God's enabling grace, can do to deal with your disagreements and to curb your conflicts.

Marital Misunderstandings, Disagreements, and Conflicts

It is helpful to make a distinction between misunderstandings, disagreements, and conflicts. The differentiation enables us to discuss the causes and solutions of each without confusing one with the other.

Misunderstandings are the occasions when couples fail to understand one another, the causes of which were explained in the previous chapter.

Disagreements are the occasions when couples are not of the same opinion on a particular issue. Like diplomats or negotiators, however, they are able to discuss their differences in a reasonably calm, self-controlled manner.

Conflicts are the occasions when couples quarrel, fight, or battle in some manner, ranging from heated verbal arguments to actual physical violence. In a conflict the disagreement escalates from a diversity of opinions to a limited or all-out war. The couple's focus shifts from attacking the problem of their differences to attacking one another. Married love that does not want to hurt one's partner gives way to the urge to win and to conquer no matter what it takes. Contrary to the Fifth Commandment, the couple inflict emotional, and in the worst cases physical, hurt on each other.

Our goal as a Christian husband and wife is to discuss our differences as disagreements without losing control of ourselves and letting those disagreements become conflicts complete with battle screams and hand grenades. We want to work through our disagreements in a loving

Christian manner so that we may reach a mutually acceptable solution which benefits our marriage.

Two Elements of Your Disagreements

Two elements are involved in your disagreements. The first is the issue of the moment. The potential issues are endless. They may be such simple and often foolish matters as how to bag the garbage or such complicated issues as Christian parenting or your family budget.

The second critical element of your disagreements is you yourselves. The kind of spirit you and your spouse bring into the situation affects the nature of your disagreements.

If you bring primarily your sinful nature with its self-interest, its evil intentions and behavior, and its passionate outbursts, your disagreements will be heated conflicts. When your sinful nature is on the loose, it arouses strife, jealousy, outbursts of anger, disputes, foul language, bitterness, slander, and yelling (cf. Galatians 5:19,20; Ephesians 4:29-31).

But if you bring primarily a civic righteousness which is in control of your emotions, your disagreements will likely be couched in a righteous language and behavior toward one another. Civic righteousness means an awareness of God's law written in your hearts and a conscience which then governs your conduct and speech to do what is right (Romans 2:14,15).

If you are governed primarily by your new spiritual nature, your disagreements will be ruled by love and never escalate into heated conflicts. For your new spiritual nature is dedicated to solely loving God and one another according to God's commandments. The more that spiritual nature is in charge during your disagreements, the more patient, calm, self-controlled, polite, kind, and loving you will be.

Regardless of the issue, by the ability the Holy Spirit gives you, you will want to bring your new Christian spirit into dealing with your disagreements and curbing your conflicts.

Reasons You May Have Marital Disagreements

A couple may have disagreements for a number of reasons such as self-interest, maladjustment, the nature of their marital personality, differing perceptions, varied backgrounds, and the issues themselves which arise.

Self-interest may shade the way one or both of you want to handle an issue. Without necessarily realizing it, you may selfishly think of meeting your own desire or goal in the matter. That takes precedence over looking out for your partner's interests. A disagreement may then develop.

Maladjustment may lead to disagreements, especially if you are newlyweds. I encourage newlyweds to give themselves at least five years to adjust to one another, for both of them have their own opinions on almost everything from apartment hunting to decorating the Christmas tree. To begin, they must decide who will sleep on which side of the bed, how to decorate their apartment, where to spend the holidays — and the list goes on endlessly. These are all potential issues of disagreement. Therefore, in the first years of marriage particularly, maladjustment is a problem.

But for as long as you are married you need to continue adjusting to one another, because each of you will have your own ideas. For example, my wife and I have painted many rooms together during our thirty-plus years of marriage. More than once I have had one idea how to clear out a room and get ready to paint it, while my wife has had another. We found ourselves disagreeing over how to proceed before we even got started. Such disagreements plague couples throughout their marriage, requiring a continuing process of adjustment and acceptance.

Your varied backgrounds may also lead to marital disagreements, because you may bring into the issues different moral, spiritual, and economic values and standards. For example, a wife had a Christian day school education, while her husband had received a public school education. The wife believes a Christian education is what is best for their children, but her husband fails to see the value of such an education and wants their children to go to a public school. When the time comes for their children to start school, they do not agree on which school to send their children to.

Finally, issues bring about marital disagreements. Situations may arise affecting the life and environment of both of you. In those instances, each of you feels the need to control your life and environment. But sometimes your needs conflict with one another. The issues themselves are potentially limitless, but here is an example of what can happen: a husband feels he must keep the job he has, even if it means being transferred to the other side of the country, but his wife feels she must remain where they are because her roots are there.

Your Disagreements Will Be Ties or Tears

Jesus said, " 'The two will become one flesh.' So they are no longer two, but one" (Mark 10:8). In marriage your lives touch and come together so you are one. But when you disagree over some point, on that point the two of you cease to be one, for your minds and wills are not united.

What you do with that disagreement will determine whether it becomes a tie or a tear in your relationship. If you do not settle that disagreement, it comes between you at that point of your lives and tears you apart. On the other hand, if you reach an agreement, it ties you together at that point of your lives. The agreement actually ties your relationship together where it had not been together before. It makes your relationship more strongly bound than it was previously. For

> What scissors do to paper,
> Unresolved disagreements do to marriages;
> But what bindings do to hands,
> Agreements do to spouses.

The less you settle your disagreements, the more little tears you will have in your relationship. Over the years you can accumulate so many little tears that they literally rip your marriage apart. You are no longer one but two again. On the other hand, the more you settle your disagreements, the more your relationship is tied together. Every issue you settle binds you together where you had not been together before. Furthermore, the more ties that bind you together, the more you are one and the less likely it will ever be that you will be torn apart.

Living disagreements are the tombstones of dead and dying marriages. Couples of troubled marriages have their ongoing, unresolved problems and disagreements. Resentment arises in their hearts and drives out their feelings of love for one another. At the end their hearts cry out the epitaph to their marriage: "We don't love one another anymore!"

Don't let your disagreements tear you apart. Settle your disagreements to tie yourselves more closely together. In the process you will strengthen the bonds that unite you.

The Reason You May Have Marital Conflicts

Have you and your partner ever had a heated argument over next to nothing and later wondered what it was all about and how it happened in the first place? When I asked that question in one of my marriage seminars, I noted quite a few grins among the husbands and wives present. It probably happens on occasion in your relationship too, does it not?

In my opinion, the majority of heated arguments in good marriages are over silly little things like how to hang the toilet paper in the bathroom. I also believe a great many arguments in good marriages begin as a simple misunderstanding of who did or said what and why. The misunderstanding leads to a disagreement, and the disagreement is fueled into a heated conflict by emotional stress, tension, irritability, or a spiritual weakness that leads to a loss of self-control.

Spiritual growth in love, patience, and understanding will do much to curtail such conflicts. From a strictly human standpoint, the following tactics will help: First, feed back and clarify what was meant or intended, as we discussed in the previous chapter. Second, drop it. It probably is not worth arguing about in the first place. Third, stay in touch with your moods. If you know you are irritable and tense, be careful that your sinful nature does not suddenly use the least provocation to vent your pent-up passions. That is especially the time to bite your tongue and get off by yourself for a while.

> As day's heat sparks the thunderstorms,
> So spouse's passions ignite marital feuds.

But maybe your disagreements regularly end up as stormy conflicts. What causes that? Let us recognize that your stormy conflicts are sinful. They arise because your sinful natures gain the upper hand. Galatians 5:19,20 states, "The acts of the sinful nature are obvious: . . . hatred, discord, jealousy, fits of rage, selfish ambition, dissensions, factions and envy." All such acts of your sinful natures may be present in your marital conflicts.

The word "hatred" describes how you and your spouse feel in the midst of your heated conflicts. The Greek word for "hatred" literally means "enmity."[1] During your conflicts you probably feel hostility and antagonism in your relationship.

The Greek word for "discord" means "strife, contention, wrangling."[2] In the plural it means "quarrels." All of those words appropriately describe your conflicts.

The Greek word for "fits of rage" means "anger, wrath, and rage."[3] Is it not true you feel anger in the midst of your heated conflicts?

The Greek word for "dissensions" means "divisions."[4] In your conflicts you are indeed divided and on opposite sides.

I do not know how severe the conflicts in your marriage become. Whatever their severity, the following is true to the extent it describes them: *Your sinful natures are responsible* for the angry yelling and screaming; the knockdown, drag-out quarrels and fights; the name-calling, dish-throwing, door-slamming battles; the verbal and maybe physical abuse; the sarcasm and cutting remarks — that tear your marriage to shreds!

Your conflicts are a no-win situation. You lose — because of the personal hurt the two of you inflict on one another, a hurt that cannot be erased or easily forgotten, a hurt that arouses further resentment and drives out your feelings of love for one another. Proverbs 18:19 says, "An

100

offended brother is more unyielding than a fortified city, and disputes are like the barred gates of a citadel." You lose — because frequently there is no winner of your conflicts. The issues remain unresolved. Finally, you lose — because God will judge you for your sinful conduct during your conflicts.

Learn to disagree lovingly in a reasonably calm, self-controlled manner to eliminate those conflicts. Your conflicts result from your sinful natures being let loose; therefore, repentance is called for to hold it in check (see chapter 4). Because you remain sinners throughout your life, however, you will never gain perfect control of your sinful natures. Occasionally you will slip, and your sinful natures will rear their ugly heads to turn your disagreement into a conflict. But as the Holy Spirit enables you to put off your past sins responsible for your conflicts, as he causes you to grow in the fruits of the Spirit — you will prevent more and more of your disagreements from turning into sinful conflicts. In the process, you will grow in the Lord and improve your marriage, deepening the love between you.

Agree to Disagree Lovingly: A Christian Approach for Dealing with Disagreements and Curbing Conflicts

I would now like to share with you a Christian approach to dealing with your disagreements and curbing your conflicts. I will assume you are both Christians who, by the renewing power of the Holy Spirit, can reach a God-pleasing understanding on how you will disagree in the future. This is the approach: both of you agree to fulfill the law of love for God and one another during your future disagreements. You agree to disagree lovingly.

First, agree to make the Word of God a regular part of your daily life both at home and in your congregation. This is an important agreement, for through the power of God's word and Spirit you will grow in the spiritual love so necessary for fulfilling the law of love and for eliminating your sinful words and actions during your disagreements. That will curb your conflicts. What is more, by his word the Holy Spirit enables you to grow in his fruits: love, peace, patience, kindness, goodness, faithfulness, gentleness and self-control (Galatians 5:22,23). Those fruits will also enable you to disagree lovingly and in the process curb your conflicts.

Agree to talk about your problems and settle them quickly in order to be reconciled to one another. Our Lord tells you to do this (cf. Matthew 5:23-25; 18:15). Neither pretending that nothing is wrong when something is nor retreating into silence carries out this instruction or solves your problems.

Agree to choose your disagreements wisely. For love's sake, abandon the quarrel before it starts. Our Lord says, "Starting a quarrel is like breaching a dam; so drop the matter before a dispute breaks out" (Proverbs 17:14). He also says, "There is a time for everything, and a season for every activity under heaven . . . a time to be silent and a time to speak" (Ecclesiastes 3:1,7).

Many little aggravations are not worth arguing about, nor are they a real problem. Maybe your wife is not the best housekeeper, maybe your husband does not always pick up after himself — but do you want to start an argument or World War III over it? No one is perfect. In love overlook those little faults and annoyances. Forgive instead of making big issues and confrontations out of them. Our Lord says, "Above all, love each other deeply, because love covers over a multitude of sins" (1 Peter 4:8).

Agree to apply, by the assistance of the Holy Spirit, spiritual love to the way you disagree. This addresses the second element of your disagreements, the spirit you and your spouse bring into them. In love you want to attack the problem, not your partner.

1 Corinthians 13:4-7 reveals how love acts in our relationship with one another. In the following paragraphs we will apply this gift of spiritual love to the subject of agreeing to disagree lovingly. But the following points could be applied to all of our marital communication just as well, as I mentioned in the preceding chapter.

> Love is patient, love is kind. It does not envy, it does not boast, it is not proud. It is not rude, it is not self-seeking, it is not easily angered, it keeps no record of wrongs. Love does not delight in

evil but rejoices with the truth. It always protects, always trusts, always hopes, always perseveres. (1 Corinthians 13:4-7)

Love is patient. The Greek word means "to have patience, wait, be patient and forbearing."[5] May your spiritual love lead you to agree to be patient. Scripture says there is a time to be silent and a time to speak. Agree that each of you will wait to pick the right time and place to discuss an issue that is on your mind. You will take the other's moods into consideration first. If you are the husband and you see your wife is going through her premenstrual irritability, you will patiently wait for another time to discuss the purchases on the charge card.

Have you ever had the experience that your spouse could not see the point you were trying to make? If you have, did you not feel frustration and anger arise within you? Agree, then, when that occurs to either of you, you will refrain from expressing that anger. Instead you will patiently explain your point again. Loving patience can prevent the anger which will intensify your disagreement.

Let your love also agree to be patient listeners. You will not interrupt one another or jump to the wrong conclusions, as we discussed in the preceding chapter.

Love is kind. The word "kind" in the Greek means "to be loving, to be merciful."[6] Agree that your spiritual love will show kindness and mercy in what you say and do. So speak in the first person "I." Say the unpleasant things about one another's faults in the kindest possible way. Do not purposely irritate one another during your disagreements.

Love does not envy. The Greek word is the verb *zeloi.* Its basic meanings are: "1) to burn with zeal, to be heated or to boil with envy, hatred, anger; 2) to desire earnestly, pursue."[7] Love does not envy someone who has what we do not have. Love is content and satisfied with the circumstances as they are and rejoices in the good fortune of the other person. In marital disagreements a Christian husband or wife will know when not to pursue a matter further but to drop the subject. Some spouses never know when to quit. May you agree not to keep pushing and harping about a matter long after it is time to call it quits.

Love does not boast. The Greek word means "to boast, to brag".[8] It has the meaning of being vain-glorious, a brag-gart.[9]

Agree to love one another by not boasting about how good you are — much better than your spouse. You will not say something like, "If it wasn't for me, this marriage would have fallen apart a long time ago! Who sees to it the children receive some love and attention around here? I do!" Agree that your love will avoid using superlatives to puff yourself up at the expense of tearing your mate down. "I never do that! You always do that!" May your love also agree not to talk as though you are so much smarter than your spouse. "How could you be so dumb? I know what is best for this family. What do you know about it?"

In all your discussions treat your mate as your equal and complement, not as your child who must be re-dressed and shaped up by you.

Love is not proud. The Greek word means "to become puffed up, conceited, to put on airs and be proud."[10] This negative trait is closely associated with the boasting men-tioned above.

May the Lord bless you with this love so that you are humble and not conceited or puffed up. Blessed with this love, agree to look at things objectively and admit when you are wrong. Consider that your spouse may know what he is talking about too and may not be just a know-it-all who refuses to listen, for you understand there is a chance you could be wrong and not realize it.

Love is not rude. The Greek word means "to behave dis-gracefully, dishonorably and indecently;[11] to act unbe-comingly."[12]

Filled with this love, agree that you will not behave dis-gracefully and dishonorably while you are disagreeing. You will not be sarcastic. Neither of you will use foul lan-guage or slander the other with filthy names. Your love will prove itself by speaking respectfully to one another and by exhibiting a God-pleasing behavior throughout your discussions.

Love is not self-seeking. A literal translation of the Greek is: "(Love) does not seek things for itself." The Greek verb is *zeteo,* which primarily means "to seek or look for in order to find."[13] In this passage it means "to strive for, aim at, desire;[14] to seek to further the profit or advantage of oneself." This word describes the selfish desire to gain what a person believes is for his own best advantage. In love, then, agree that you will not be ruled by your own self-interests. You will listen to your partner's concerns. Each of you will try to see the issues as your partner does.

Love is not easily angered. The Greek word means "to become irritated, angry."[15] The next chapter will address how love works to curb and remove anger. But for now let me urge you to agree to remain calm, resist feelings of irritation, and not raise your voices in passionate outbursts. Anger will only inhibit your ability to talk through your disagreements to mutual resolutions.

Love keeps no record of wrongs. A literal translation of the Greek is: "(Love) does not take into account the evil thing." Christian love overlooks the evil things said or done by someone else.

In love agree to overlook during your disagreements the faults and sins your partner may slip into. You are not perfect individuals. Therefore you may slip into impatience, anger, interrupting, a poor choice of words. When that happens, you will lovingly ignore those incidents, forgive them, and go on. Love will cover a multitude of sins in communicating with one another as well as other kinds of sins (1 Peter 4:8).

May your love also agree that during your disagreements you will not bring up one another's past faults and sins. When you have addressed those sins and forgiven each other, they are finished, forgotten, and in love not to be brought up again.

Love does not delight in evil but rejoices with the truth. The Greek word for "evil" is *adikia.* It denotes "wickedness, wrongdoing, unrighteousness."[16] The Greek word for "truth" is *aletheia.* It may refer to God's word, and more narrowly to the religious and moral truths expounded in God's word. The love awakened by the Holy Spirit is never in favor of any kind of wickedness or wrongdoing. It is always on the side of what God's word says .

In every aspect of your life and marriage, including how you talk to one another, may Christian love lead you to frown on what is evil and to stand for what is right according to God's word. In your conduct with one another, in your speaking to one another, in your treatment of one another — at all times you will desire to uphold the moral law of God which is summarized: "Love one another."

The word "truth" in the above passage includes the Lord's law to speak only the truth to one another. In love, then, agree not to talk in glowing generalities about your mate's faults. If you are the wife, don't say to your husband he always leaves his clothes lying all over the house, when the truth is once in a while he leaves his socks by the side of the bed. I have frequently asked a spouse who has made some general type of accusation about his partner to cite specific instances to substantiate it. Agree that before either of you accuse the other, you will be able to point out a few instances that substantiate the accusation.

Love always protects, always trusts, always hopes. The word "always" in the Greek is *panta*, which may be better translated "all things." The word "protects" is the Greek verb *stegei*. This verb can mean "to cover over with silence; to keep secret; to hide and conceal," in order to protect someone else.[17] The meaning, then, is that Christian love keeps the errors and faults of another secret. It does not relate them or gossip about them to anyone else. The verb *stegei* can also mean "to cover by keeping off" whatever is a threat.[18] It therefore means "to bear up against," and "to endure."[19,20] The meaning would then be Christian love endures the errors and faults of others.

Love conceals to protect another. Therefore, let the love of each of you agree to keep confidential what your mate says in your discussions and what your mate's faults are. You each need this assurance: Whatever you say to one another in the privacy of your marriage, whatever faults you may have in your marriage — will not be passed on to outside parties. Such gossip hurts the partner who is being talked about. Furthermore, it will discourage the intimate conversations so necessary for a good marriage. For how can a spouse feel free to talk intimately with his partner when he is afraid his partner is going to repeat it to someone else?

The Greek word for "trusts" in the above passage means "to continue to believe."[21] The Greek word for "hopes" means "to continue to hope for, expect."[22] Spiritual love, then, continues to believe and to expect the best in the other person.

In love agree that you will believe what your spouse tells you. Such mutual trust is a bedrock of your marriage. This agreement may seem unnecessary to many couples, because they have always believed one another. But to couples who are trying to patch up their troubled marriage, this agreement is absolutely necessary. If you are one of those couples trying to patch up your marriage, it is especially important that you believe one another in the present and not judge one another's statements on the basis of the past.

May you also agree that in everything, especially during your disagreements, you will put the best construction on what your mate says and does — trusting and hoping your partner is saying and doing what is right with the best of intentions. Where such trust and hope are missing, suspicions arise to the detriment of your relationship.

Agree to Settle Your Disagreements with an Agreement

This addresses the first element of your disagreements, the issue over which you have different opinions. This final agreement turns your disagreements into ties which bind you closer together; failure to reach an agreement turns your disagreements into tears which pull you apart. Especially on issues of a serious nature affecting your lives and future, before the two of you decide what to do, take it to the Lord in prayer. Ask him to guide you to the right decision and final agreement.

Following are methods for reaching a mutual agreement:

Capitulation

One of you gives in to the other on the issue at hand. In a loving relationship each of you will give in at times for the sake of the other, for your Christian love will want to do what is best for your mate. Furthermore, if you are the husband, you will want to give in to your wife's wishes because you love your wife with a self-sacrificial love. If you are the wife, you will want to give in to your husband because you are a submissive wife, who arrange yourself under your husband.

Compromise

Both of you give in a little to reach an acceptable agreement for the reasons stated above, or agree on an alternative which is not exactly what either of you had in mind but which is acceptable to you both.

Acceptance

Each of you accepts the fact you have an irreconcilable difference of opinion on that issue, and you agree to leave it at that and live with it. Couples of different religions and political views, for example, may need to do this.

Cast Lots

This sounds odd to our sophisticated minds of the twentieth century, but it is a scriptural practice that worked well in biblical times. It is written, "Casting the lot settles disputes and keeps strong opponents apart" (Proverbs 18:18). What is wrong with flipping a coin to decide whether you go to dinner or to see a movie, for example?

Be Reconciled after Your Disagreement

Agree that each of you will apologize afterwards for any sins you may commit against one another during your disagreement. Agree also to forgive one another for those sins. Finally, agree to seal your resolution with a kiss. If, in spite of your best Christian intentions to disagree lovingly, your disagreement had turned into an argument, remember, kissing and making up is the best part — don't cheat yourselves out of that!

Endnotes

1. Greek *echthrai;* Joseph Henry Thayer, *Greek-English Lexicon of the New Testament,* (Grand Rapids, Michigan: Zondervan Publishing House, 1975), p 265.

2. Greek *eris; Ibid.,* p 249.

3. Greek *thumoi;* F. Wilbur Gingrich, *Shorter Lexicon of the Greek New Testament,* (Chicago and London: The University of Chicago Press, 1973), p 96.

4. Greek *dichostasiai;* Thayer: p 153.

5. Greek *makrothumei;* Gingrich: p 130.

6. Greek *chresteuetai; Ibid.,* p 237

7. Thayer: p 271.

8. Greek *perpereuetai;* Gingrich: p 171

9. Thayer: p 507

10. Greek *phusioutai;* Gingrich: p 232.

11. Greek *aschemonei; Ibid.,* p 31.

12. Thayer: p 82.

13. *Ibid.,* p 272.

14. Gingrich: pp 90,91.

15. Greek *paroxunetai; Ibid.,* p 164.

16. *Ibid.,* p 4.

17. Thayer: p 586.

18. *Ibid.,* 586.

19. *Ibid.,* 586.

20. Gingrich: p 202.

21. Greek *pisteuei; Ibid.,* p 173.

22. Greek *elpizei; Ibid.,* p 67.

7.

RESOLVING ANGER AND RESENTMENT

Anger in a marriage is like the sun in the sky —
It never stops rising
So eliminating anger in a marriage is like rooting out
weeds in a field —
It is a never-ending job.

A Definition of Anger

Scripture reveals that anger is a response to what someone else says or does. "When Rachel . . . said to Jacob, 'Give me children, or I'll die!' Jacob became angry with her and said, 'Am I in the place of God, who has kept you from having children?' " (Genesis 30:1,2). In Exodus 32:19 Moses' righteous anger was aroused by the Israelites making a golden calf. Proverbs 15:1 reveals anger may be a response to what someone else says; "A gentle answer turns away wrath, but a harsh word stirs up anger." In numerous passages we read that the Lord's anger was aroused by what his people had done.

Anger is a reaction or a response to our perception of what is happening around us or to us, particularly to the words and actions of others or to circumstances which arise in our life. Anger becomes lingering resentment and bitterness toward someone when it is not dispelled by resolving what caused it. Resentment in turn often hinders reconciliation with another person.

Causes of Anger

Frustration

When your will and goals are blocked, frustration arises, and this causes you to feel angry. The greater the number of your goals, plans, desires, needs, and expectations, the more frequently you experience that they are blocked and thwarted. When this happens, you feel frustrated and angry. In addition, the more intense your determination is to achieve your personal goals and desires, the greater your frustration and anger when they are denied.

Has it ever happened, after you had prepared your list of things you had to get done on a certain day, that from the very beginning nothing went right? You became caught up in one problem after another and experienced one setback after another and one hour started to slip into another and what you had set out to do was not getting done before you had to leave for an appointment you could not miss — a-n-d what happened? The more setbacks you had and the faster the time was slipping away, the more frustrated you became — until you started to burn and fume. You were hot! You perhaps were ready to blow up at the first one who said anything to you. That is one type of frustration you and your spouse must learn to contend with in your marriage.

Now let's look at some types of frustration that may be a direct result of your marital relationship. If you try hard to please your mate but he or she is continually critical of you, if you are a wife whose husband has used you over the years to satisfy his own sexual desires without giving you the love you need — you probably have been and are frustrated and angry. When you cannot convince your mate of your point of view on a particular issue, when you cannot get your mate to understand what you are trying to explain, when you are not permitted to address and work out your marital problems — you probably experience frustration and anger. When your partner has no desire to work at improving and saving your marriage, when your partner says he will change for the better to save your marriage but he continues to do what has been destroying your marriage — and your problems remain as bad as ever — you probably experience frustration and anger. What is more, as your frustration and anger rise, your feelings of love subside. Obviously, the way to eliminate this type of frustration and anger is to clear up the underlying problems that are causing them.

Self-Interest

The naturally sinful hearts of husbands and wives, even of those who are Christians, cause them at times to want what they want when they want it. Because sin has so thoroughly corrupted the nature and mind of all human beings, they may not realize at the time that their goals and desires are selfish. They are merely doing what comes so naturally to them — looking out first for their own self-interests. That natural inclination exists in us all, in you as well as in me. Ungratified self-interests, then, may at times be the underlying cause of frustration and anger in your marriage. James wrote,

> What is the source of quarrels and conflicts among you? Is not the source your pleasures that wage war in your members? You lust and do not have; so you commit murder. And you are envious and cannot obtain; so you fight and quarrel. (James 4:1,2 NASB)

When one of you experiences your self-interests, desires, or plans blocked by the other, you may become frustrated and angry with your spouse. For example, a wife planned to finish making her dress on Saturday morning in time for the wedding reception that evening. She planned on her husband taking their daughter to her Saturday morning piano lesson while she worked on her dress. But her husband had made plans to go fishing. When they start to discuss their plans for Saturday morning, they both become frustrated and angry over the possibility of having to change their plans.

What will eliminate your anger resulting from frustrated self-interests? Love that is willing to yield and give in for the sake of your spouse, as we discussed in chapter 4.

A Hardening of the Heart

Anger may arise when one spouse rejects his partner's proper rebuke of his sin. Instead of repenting of his sinful behavior and admitting he was wrong, he impenitently resents his partner's rebuke and becomes angry.

Unloving Injustice and Sin

A spouse may be aroused to anger by the sinful treatment he suffers at the hands of his mate. If you have ever been the target of your mate's nasty remark or other abusive behavior, you probably became angry with him.

False Perceptions

Chapter 5 explained how erring perceptions bring about misunderstandings and unwarranted anger in your marriage.

A Bad Temper

A bad temper is a learned habit. Proverbs 22:24,25 says, "Do not make friends with a hot-tempered man, do not associate with one easily angered, or you may learn his ways and get yourself ensnared."

In marital counseling I have observed that the bad temper of a spouse was often learned from his or her parents. An adult, however, may also have acquired a bad temper during his childhood through learning that his temper tantrums succeeded in getting him what he wanted.

Is Anger Always Wrong? Is It Ever Right?

Christians may think anger is always wrong. But the rightness or the wrongness of anger depends on the cause of the anger and how the anger is then released.

Some anger is right. Ephesians 4:26 tells us, "Be angry, and yet do not sin" (NASB). This passage makes it clear that it is possible to be angry and not be guilty of sin in the process.

Anger can be a correct response. In the Scriptures we learn even our holy God is aroused to wrath by people's injustice, wickedness, and sin. God himself is holy and without sin, so we know his anger is always right and never wrong. Romans 1:18 states, "The wrath of God is being revealed from heaven against all the godlessness and wickedness of men who suppress the truth by their wickedness" (cf. also Ephesians 5:5,6).

Our sinless Lord Jesus exhibited a righteous anger during his earthly ministry too. When the Pharisees condemned his showing mercy and doing good on the Sabbath day, "He looked around at them in anger," and was "deeply distressed at their stubborn hearts" (Mark 3:5). Jesus' righteous anger also led him to make a whip out of cords and drive the money changers and merchants out of the temple.

Since the Lord is just, his anger over injustice and sin is a justified anger. Christian people today also demonstrate righteous anger at times. When they see injustice, oppression, and wickedness, they become angry. Their anger motivates them to correct the injustices. For example, a parent's godly anger may motivate him to discipline his older child for mistreating his younger child.

Anger is right, then, when it is aroused by injustice and sin and the angry person desires to see righteousness prevail, as Jesus did. Furthermore, anger is right when it is directed at correcting the injustice and sin, as Jesus did.

But usually anger in marriages is wrong. Anger is wrong when it arises from the frustration of having a goal or selfish desire blocked and ungratified. Like a spoiled child, a spouse becomes angry because he cannot have his own way.

That anger is a sinful emotion. Selfishness is a love of self, which arouses selfish desires and behavior. Such self-love, or selfishness, replaces loving concern for others. But Jesus commanded us to love one another and told us how we are to do this. He said, "A new command I give you: Love one another. As I have loved you, so you must love one another" (John 13:34). We are to love one another as Jesus loved us — self-sacrificially and unselfishly. Therefore, anger in marriage that stems from a frustrated self-ishness or self-love is a strong emotion that is opposed to carrying out Jesus' command to love one's spouse. In such an instance anger is a sinful emotion.

Anger is wrong also when it is released destructively to hurt someone else verbally or physically. Such anger is a sin against the Fifth Commandment.

Jesus addressed this kind of sinful, angry verbal abuse when he preached on the meaning of the Fifth Commandment. Jesus said,

> You have heard that it was said to the people long ago, "Do not murder, and anyone who murders will be subject to judgment." But I tell you that anyone who is angry with his brother (without cause) will be subject to judgment. Again, anyone who says to his brother, "Raca," [an Aramaic term of abuse possibly meaning "empty head," or "air head" in today' s terminology[1]] is answerable to the Sanhedrin. But anyone who says, "You fool!" will be in danger of the fire of hell. (Matthew 5:21,22)

Jesus' sermon on the Fifth Commandment reveals that when anyone releases angry verbal abuse on another person and uses rude names and words to humiliate that other person, he will be held guilty and punished under that commandment. Verbal abuse is also forbidden in Ephesians 4:29: "Do not let any unwholesome talk ["rotten word," literally] come out of your mouths." Colossians 3:8 tells us to put aside slander and filthy or abusive language.

The bad temper usually associated with verbal and even physical abuse is also forbidden. Proverbs 22:24,25 tells us not to associate with a hot-tempered man, lest we learn his ways and find ourselves ensnared by them .

When anger arises from erring perceptions, it is also wrong. This is an unjustified anger, for it stems from the angry person's own error and not from any sin on the part of the one he is angry with.

Anger is wrong too when it arises from an unwillingness to accept a rebuke for a sin. I mentioned before that this anger stems from a hardened heart. Proverbs 9:7 describes this kind of anger: "Whoever corrects a mocker invites insult; whoever rebukes a wicked man incurs abuse."

Finally, anger is wrong when it simmers as resentment, hatred, and the desire to take revenge. Ephesians 4:26,31 (NASB) says, "Do not let the sun go down on your anger. . . . Let all bitterness . . . be put away from you, along with all malice" (the Greek word for malice also means "ill-will and malignity or a desire to injure"[2]).

The Results of Anger

Correction, abuse, and a breakdown in communication are three common results of anger in a marriage.

Correction

Anger may lead one of you to correct the unloving treatment and sin of the other. If you are hurt by an unkind, sarcastic remark, a resulting anger may move you to rebuke your mate for it. The purpose of your rebuke is to correct your erring partner, to lead him to repent and to apologize for it. If it accomplishes this, the matter is settled and your marriage goes on.

But be careful of this: do not let your anger over being mistreated turn into lashing out with a nasty remark to hurt your mate, so he knows how he hurt you. That is revenge, not a proper rebuke of sin to correct an erring partner.

Jesus left us this example to follow when we have been mistreated or slandered: quietly endure it because that pleases God. "When they hurled their insults at him, he did not retaliate; when he suffered, he made no threats" (1 Peter 2:23). The Greek word for "hurled insults at" means "to reproach, rail at, revile, heap abuse upon."[3] That is what the Jews and thieves did to Jesus. But Jesus did not "retaliate," that is reciprocate with abuse of his own, which is the meaning of the Greek word.[4] May that be an example to you not to retaliate in anger with abusive words of your own. Rebuke, yes; take revenge, no.

Abuse

Contrary to the Fifth Commandment, anger frequently results in verbal and/or physical abuse in a marriage. Is this sinful misuse of anger present in your marriage? Does anger erupt into yelling at one another or calling one another names? Does anger spew out profanity? Does your anger boil over into slanderous attacks on one another's person or past? Does anger explode into one of you slapping or hitting the other? If any of those things happen in your marriage, you are guilty of the sinful misuse of anger.

A Breakdown in Communication

When anger arises, meaningful, constructive communication ceases. Has anger halted your communication? Have you and your spouse been unable to talk out your problems because you have regularly become angry with one another? Have you started to talk, then gotten mad at one another, and your attempts to communicate ended — in anger?

H. Norman Wright in his book *Communication: Communication: Communication: Key To Your Marriage* quoted David Augsburger on the use of anger and the effects anger has on the angry person himself. The angry person becomes vulnerable, his self-control is at a minimum, his ability to think clearly is impaired, and his common sense is lost.[5] Scripture corroborates that observation: "A quick-tempered man does foolish things" (Proverbs 14:17). In addition, the person's anger may quickly turn into resentment, hatred, malice, and violence.[6] Scripture describes those traits as the deeds of the sinful nature (Galatians 5:20; Ephesians 4:29-32).

This is why your communication breaks down, then, when you become angry with one another; each of you falls to a low point of self-control; you then say or do things you otherwise would not and which you may later regret. Each of you has your ability to think clearly impaired; you then have difficulty putting your thoughts into words. You may get your words switched around or stammer in incomplete sentences. Thus you fail to communicate clearly. At the same time, because your ability to think clearly is impaired, each of you has greater difficulty following your mate's line of thought and understanding how he is seeing the issue. Each of you loses your common sense, and on the spur of that angry moment you may decide on a course of action you would not take if you had your wits about you. That in turn may further confuse or infuriate your mate. Each of you is being controlled by a strong emotion which wants to be released against the other and which does not want to listen to the other. Your anger then wants to attack your partner rather than the problem.

When the preceding things happen to both of you, your communication breaks down. Effective communication is impossible under the influence of an anger that inhibits your thinking, speaking, and listening processes and has the sole intention of lashing out to win the argument at all costs.

Let me share this with you also: if your anger turns into resentment, your resentment will also hinder constructive communication between you. Your resentment will color your perceptions of one another's words and motives. As we have seen previously, under the influence of resentment each of you will tend to perceive what you expect to perceive in and from your spouse and not understand what you should.

What People Do with Their Anger

Repress It

They refuse to acknowledge and accept their angry feelings. Repressing anger is not a God-pleasing way to deal with your anger. First, if you have been repressing your anger, it may be due to an erring conscience. You may mistakenly think all anger is wrong. But all anger is not wrong, as mentioned before. Second, your repressed anger is likely to turn into resentment, which the Lord says to put away (Ephesians 4:31). Third, if you repress your anger, you may be unable to speak truthfully to your mate and tell him when something is wrong. Repressing your anger may also prevent you from following Matthew 18:15, which directs you to talk to your mate about his sin against you. Fourth, when you repress your anger, you direct it inwardly, instead of at correcting the problem.

Ventilate It

These individuals let their anger blow up like a Mount St. Helens. They let their bad temper spew their heated anger and rage over everything and everyone around them. They yell, they use abusive language, they may even become violent.

Some modern psychologists and counselors encourage their clients to ventilate their anger to get rid of it. They advise their clients to vent their anger against someone else by pounding their fists against a wall or into a pillow, while yelling and screaming at the wall or pillow as loudly as they can. One Christian wife told me her psychologist became upset with her when she would not do those things to relieve her anger against her husband.

Such acts may bring some psychological relief, but I cannot agree with such counseling. First, it violates the Fifth Commandment by encouraging a mock murder of the other person. Second, it encourages the very things the Lord forbids — bitterness, anger, wrath, clamor, slander, and malice (Ephesians 4:31). Third, it does nothing to address the problems which caused the anger in the first place. Nor does it bring about a reconciliation. Fourth, it undermines the scriptural procedure for removing anger with another person through the forgiveness of that person's sins (Ephesians 4:32).

If you have been ventilating your anger in your marriage, not only have you violated the Fifth Commandment, you have damaged your marital relationship. You have made your partner justifiably angry with you because of your sinful conduct against him.

Stew in It

Their anger toward their spouse simmers and burns steadily in resentment and bitterness. They may clam up and refuse to talk out of a desire to punish the other person. They may refuse for days, months, even years to do anything to settle the issues and be reconciled to their spouse.

Stewing in your anger is sinful. Our Lord instructs you to talk to your partner about his sin against you (Matthew 18:15). In addition, he tells you to tell the truth to your spouse, which would include the truth about what is wrong in your marriage (Ephesians 4:25,26). What is more, he teaches you to put away your bitterness by forgiving your mate (Ephesians 4:31,32).

Redirect It

As one wife explained to me, she likes to sit down, write out her anger on paper, and throw it away afterwards. Maybe you use the energy of your anger to clean the house, or to wash the car, or to do something else.

That approach to dealing with your anger is all right as far as it goes. But while your busy-work releases the strong emotion of your anger, it does nothing toward righting the wrong that was done, nor does it do anything to bring about a reconciliation between you and your mate. Following the instructions of our Lord, after you have released your anger, you still should talk to your mate to settle the matter which caused your anger. If you do not settle that matter and become reconciled, although your initial feelings of anger may have been released, your anger may turn into resentment, in which case you end up stewing in it.

If you realize you have been repressing, ventilating, stewing in your anger, or redirecting it without becoming reconciled to your spouse afterwards — do you now think our Lord wants you to continue handling your anger in that fashion? Let's look at what our Lord teaches us about handling anger in our marriage.

Learning from the Lord to Handle Our Anger

Minimize Frustrations

We learned earlier that when our will and goals are blocked, we become frustrated and angry. But what will prevent that frustration and anger from rising in your marriage?

Learn to accept God's will for yourselves in every situation, rather than always asserting your own will. Subordinate your will to God's will at all times. Accept whatever happens as God's will for you. When you set aside your will to elevate God's will in its place, you will not feel frustrated and angry when things do not work out as you had planned.

James 4:13-17 teaches us to regard God's will for us and to realize our life and plans are entirely in his hands. To think or to say that we have it in our power to do whatever we have set our mind on is a pretentious boast. James 4:13-17 was originally addressed to Jewish converts who set their will to making money during the forthcoming year. But verse 15 reveals the principle that trusting in God's will applies to whatever Christians may have in mind. As you read these verses, substitute your daily plans in your married life for the conducting of business. Then see what the Lord instructs you to do.

> Now listen, you who say, "Today or tomorrow we will go to this or that city, spend a year there, carry on business and make money." Why, you do not even know what will happen tomorrow. What is your life? You are a mist that appears for a little while and then vanishes. Instead, you ought to say, "If it is the Lord's will, we will live and do this or that." As it is, you boast and brag. All such boasting is evil. (James 4:13-16)

Perhaps you can see now that if you and your spouse make your individual plans contingent on whether God wants them to be fulfilled, you will not become frustrated and angry when they are not. You will have accepted in advance the possibility that the Lord may have other plans for you.

To eliminate the frustration resulting from your ungratified self-interests, may each of you be moved to repent of your self-interests, as we discussed in chapter 4.

And here is a practical solution to reducing frustration in your married life: do not plan or schedule too many things into the short space of one day. Then, if you experience some setbacks along the way, you will not become frustrated about all the things you are unable to get done.

Learn Self-Control

Self-control is a fruit of the Spirit (Galatians 5:22,23). It enables us to restrain ourselves. This virtue masters our desires and passions, including our anger. Spiritual growth in the fruits of the Spirit through the regular use of God's word is therefore a most important part of our learning to control our anger.

Armed with this gift of self-control, may you remain conscious of your emotions. As soon as you begin to feel angry with your spouse, speak the truth in love and kindness. Admit you are beginning to feel angry. Inform your spouse of your anger in as inoffensive a manner as possible. Here again it will help if you talk about yourself in the first person "I," rather than accusing your partner in the second person "you." "I am feeling angry" is likely to have better results than "You are making me angry."

When you admit you are angry, explain the cause of your anger. Then let your partner clarify what he said or did. This is the process of feedback and clarification described earlier.

Direct the Energy at the Problem

As we noted before, anger is right when it arises in response to injustice and sin and its energy is directed at correcting that injustice and sin. That is how Scripture says the Lord uses his anger. Let us learn from him to use our anger in the same way.

We may use the energy of our anger in several ways to correct the problem that aroused it. We may use it to clear up erring perceptions and misunderstandings through the process of feedback and clarification. Or we may direct the energy of our anger at correcting our mate's sin to lead him to repentance and in the process bring about a reconciliation between us. Our purpose is not to hurt our mate but to build him up so he will do what is right (Ephesians 4:29).

Sometimes we should direct the energy of our anger at ourselves, for we were the one in the wrong. We should be angry with ourselves when we see that our anger arose from our own ungratified self-interests. In those instances

122

we need to repent. May we then say to our spouse something like, "You know, I was thinking only of myself, not of you. I'm sorry. I admit to the Lord I was wrong too, and I will pray for his forgiveness and for help to overcome my own selfish ambitions." Then there may be times when we come to see that our anger arose from our proud unwillingness to heed a proper rebuke of our sinful conduct. In such cases we might say to our mate something like, "You were right. I became angry because my own sinful and stubborn pride did not want to admit I was way off base in saying to you what I did. Please forgive me. And when I ask for the Lord's forgiveness, I will ask him to help me control my tongue."

Finally, let us learn to put off our resentment. Resentment is anger directed at another person like our spouse, but the energy of the anger burns inside of us rather than being directed at settling the matter between us. Let us use the energy of that anger to speak up about the problem in order to resolve it. If apologies and forgiveness are also expressed in the process as they should be, we will become reconciled and our resentment will disappear so the feelings of love can return. Is that not what our Lord wants? Is that not what you want as well in your marriage?

With God's Help a Bad Temper Can Be Brought Under Control

Husbands and wives have the moral responsibility to control their anger so they do not sinfully misuse it. A bad temper is a learned habit. If you have a bad temper, you need to learn with God's help to control it. Scripture reveals that a person can control his anger. Look at the following passages:

> A fool gives full vent to his anger, but a wise man keeps himself under control". (Proverbs 29:11)
>
> A man's discretion makes him slow to anger, And it is his glory to overlook a transgression." (Proverbs 19:11 NASB)

He who is slow to anger has great understanding, but he who is quick-tempered exalts folly. (Proverbs 14:29 NASB)

May the Holy Spirit lead you to repent of your bad temper. Repentance is a change of mind, in this case about sinning against God by letting your anger get the best of you.

I urge you to confess your sinful temper to the Lord in prayer and ask him to forgive you. May the Lord's gospel then enable you to believe your sin of anger has been forgiven for Jesus' sake. Why should God forgive you for Jesus' sake? First, Jesus was your substitute who kept this part of God's law perfectly for you. Jesus never sinfully misused anger, as it is written, "In him is no sin" (1 John 3:5). Second, Jesus carried your sins of anger as well as all of your other sins to the cross, where he was punished for them in your place. The Bible states, "Christ died for sins once for all, the righteous for the unrighteous, to bring you to God." "The blood of Jesus, his Son, purifies us from all sin" (1 Peter 3:18; 1 John 1:7). Therefore God has forgiven and does forgive your sin of anger. So may you be led to confess it to him and be assured of your forgiveness (1 John 1:9).

May you then in prayer ask the Lord to give you the strength by that good news of your forgiveness to control your anger. Since God's will is that you do not sin in your anger, you can be certain he will hear your prayer and answer you (1 John 5:14,15).

As a Christian redeemed through Jesus Christ, put on the full armor of God to guard against the temptation to lose your temper. Read Ephesians 6:10-17. Part of that full armor of God is the sword of the Spirit, which is the word of God. So take that sword and use it to fight off the temptation to lose your temper. Here is how you can do that: Take ¼ of a sheet of 8½ x 11 paper. Fold it in half. Then print on it the following Bible passages: James 1:19; Ephesians 4:26,29-32; 1 Corinthians 13:4-7; Romans 12:17-19,21; Proverbs 29:11. When you have made up your "Sword of the Spirit," keep it in your shirt pocket or purse. As soon as you begin to feel angry, take it out and read it through in order to remain in control of your temper.

This "Sword of the Spirit" works by the power of God. I have had counselees use it with good success. One husband who had a very bad temper since childhood used it. The last time I heard, he had not lost his temper in eighteen months at home or at work. In fact, it worked so well for him, he said he made another one and gave it to a relative who also had a bad temper.

What I have just shared with you is what Ephesians 4:22-24 calls putting off the old sinful nature that ventilated anger and putting on the new spiritual nature that controls anger. Remember, to be able to put off the old and put on the new, it is important that you grow spiritually through God's word. Grow in the word, and by the grace of God deepen the love in your marriage at the same time.

Endnotes

1. F. Wilbur Gingrich, *Shorter Lexicon of the Greek New Testament*, (Chicago and London: The University of Chicago Press, 1973), p 192.

2. Greek *kakia; Ibid.*, p 106.

3. Greek *loidoroumenos;* Joseph Henry Thayer, *Greek-English Lexicon of the New Testament*, (Grand Rapids, Michigan: Zondervan Publishing House, 1975), p 382.

4. *Ibid.*, p 50.

5. H. Norman Wright, *Communication: Communication: Communication: Key To Your Marriage*, (Ventura, California: Regal Books, 1984), p 95.

6. *Ibid.*, p 95.

7. *Ibid.*, p 90.

PART 3

Deepening Love
for
Marital Happiness

BY PROMOTING LOVE IN YOUR MARRIAGE

8.

IDENTIFYING THE TYPES OF LOVE IN YOUR MARRIAGE

Known to all, but ill-defined,
Is this thing named "Love"
That lovers call divine.
By what name do you know it?
"Sharing?"
"Caring?"
"Fondness?"
"Sex?"
"Romance?"
"Friendship?"
"Endearment?"
Is any one of these its rightful name?
Or may it be: "All!"?

I have found married and unmarried couples alike have difficulty defining what love is. "Love" is a concept that is "ill-defined" in the minds of most couples. Is that true of you as well? Before you read this chapter, I would like you to do this: you and your mate write down separately what the word "love" means to you. Then compare your answers and read on. I think you will each learn several things. First, you are likely to learn how difficult "love" is to define. Second, you are likely to learn that when you have said "I love you" to each other, the two of you did not mean the same thing. Third, through comparing your definitions you will learn what your mate means when he tells you he loves you. Fourth, as you read this chapter, you can compare your answers to what the Lord says love is and broaden your understanding of its meaning. In the process you will be able to see the love you need to have and to feel in your marriage in order to deepen the love between you.

Marriage embraces different types of love. Couples have difficulty defining "love" because our English language has only one word to describe those different concepts of love. The Hebrew and Greek of the original Scriptures, however, have several words to describe them. In this chapter we will look into the meaning of those Hebrew and Greek words to see what types of love the Lord intended for all marriages — including yours.

Love as Companionship and Friendship

Adam was alone immediately after his creation. God's solution to Adam's loneliness was to create a woman and bring her to him to be his wife. Only the close companionship and friendship of a mate could solve the problem of his loneliness.

Being close companions and friends is one type of love that is necessary for you to have a happy, satisfying marriage.

This marital love as friends and companions is also revealed in the Song of Solomon. In 5:16 the bride says of her bridegroom: "This is my lover, this my friend." The Hebrew word means a friend or companion.[1] Likewise the bridegroom in 1:9,15 calls his bride, "My darling." The word "darling" in the Hebrew means "a female friend, a beloved female."[2]

Titus 2: 4 also reveals God intends you to enjoy the love of companionship and friendship in your marriage. "Then they can train the younger women to love their husbands." The Greek word for "love their husbands" is *philandrous*. It is a compound word from the words *phileo* and *aner*. Aner means "a man, or a husband."[3] *Phileo* is a verb which means "to love, to be friendly to someone."[4]

We are able to obtain a better understanding of the nature of this love a wife is to have for her husband by looking at other verses in which *phileo* is used. When we look at Matthew 10:37; John 11:3; 20:2; 21:15-17, for example, we find *phileo* denotes a natural and warm affection for someone else.

The Greek adjective *philos* is related to the verb *phileo*. *Philos* means "to be kindly disposed and devoted to someone else."[5] When it is used as a noun, it is the Greek word for "friend."[6]

From the preceding we have learned the Greek word *philandrous* in Titus 2:4 means the wife is to love her husband as a friend; she is to be a friend and companion to her husband. In every marriage, then, yours as well, God intends the couple to enjoy this love of companionship and friendship. This is an emotional love that feels a natural, warm affection for the other partner in the marriage.

This love as close friends and companions will enable you to share with one another the intimate things that you would not and cannot share with others, and that deepen the love between you. Your love as friends will make it possible for your marriage to be the sharing relationship that God made marriage in the beginning.

In chapter 1 we also observed that God made marriage a sociable relationship. Your love as friends and companions will also make your marriage such a sociable relationship. As the best of friends, you will spend enjoyable time doing things together. That too will deepen the love between you.

Love as a Sense of Belonging to One Another

While Adam was alone after his creation, the Lord had him name the various creatures. As he gave all those creatures appropriate names, Adam learned that, unlike them, he did not have a helper and companion. But when he saw the woman the Lord had created for him, he said, "This is now bone of my bones and flesh of my flesh; she shall be called 'woman,' for she was taken out of man" (Genesis 2:23). Adam realized that woman belonged together with him. She was his helper, companion, and complement. She corresponded to him.

That sense of belonging together is alluded to by the Hebrew word *knegdō* in Genesis 2:18, which means "suitable for him." This Hebrew word is used to indicate things which correspond to each other or are alike and are set opposite to each other for comparison,[7] such as salt and pepper shakers, for example. The word's meaning in this verse, then, is "corresponding to, counterpart." The woman was made a helper corresponding to the man. When the Lord brought the woman to Adam, he received her as one who corresponded to himself. Of all the creatures God had made, the two of them alone belonged together. God had made them a matched pair.

Genesis 2:24 also alludes to this love as a sense of belonging only to one another. "For this reason a man will leave his father and mother and be united to his wife, and they will become one flesh." The husband's and wife's feeling of belonging to one another is seen in the man's leaving his parents to be united to his wife. The word "united" in the Hebrew, *dabhāq,* literally means "to cleave to, to adhere to, to be glued together."[8]

Love in marriage as a sense of belonging together is revealed in other passages as well. In the Song of Solomon the bride says about herself and her husband, "My lover is mine and I am his" (2:16); "I am my lover's and my lover is mine" (6:3). On a number of occasions God spoke in the Old Testament of his relationship with his people in terms of his people being his wife. What existed in a marriage between a husband and wife existed, or was to exist, between God and his people. God said of his people, or wife, "And you became mine. . . . (Oholah and Oholibah) were mine. . . . Oholah engaged in prostitution while she was still mine; and she lusted after her lovers." (Ezekiel 16:8; 23:4,5).

Regarding this love as a mutual sense of belonging to one another, we can make several observations. Since those last passages in Ezekiel reveal that adultery breaks that state of belonging to one another, this love of belonging only to one another requires each to be loyal and faithful to the other. That sense of belonging to one another will also contribute to the feeling of being comfortable with one another. What is more, it will cultivate a feeling of security and safety, so that each one knows, no matter how badly things may go for him in the world at large, he will be received and taken in by his partner.

Such love as a loyalty and a refuge of security and safety is exemplified figuratively in Ezekiel 16:1-14. There the Lord spoke of his people as a woman he had taken in to be his wife. He took her in when she was despised and no one looked on her with pity or compassion. He cared for her, he washed her, he dressed her beautifully, he made her a queen.

The preceding passages have shown us that another type of love necessary for you and your spouse to have a mutually pleasing marriage is a sense of belonging only to each other. In that love you will enjoy one another's loyalty and faithfulness. You will be comfortable with one another. You will know your spouse is a refuge of safety and security, of care and concern. What is more, that love as a sense of belonging to each other will help both of you feel your relationship is a unique and committed relationship, as God made marriage.

Love as a Delight in One's Marriage Partner

When Eve was brought to Adam and they were married, Adam literally said in the Hebrew, "This one, this time, is bone of my bones and flesh of my flesh" (Genesis 2:23). Those words reveal the excitement, the delight, the joy he felt upon seeing the woman who became his wife. To say he was jubilant over her would not be an overstatement.

Love as a sense of joy, delight, and rapture in one's mate is also displayed in other passages. In Proverbs 5:18,19 the husband is instructed to rejoice in the wife of his youth and be captivated by her love.

> May your fountain be blessed,
> and may you rejoice in the wife of your youth.
> A loving doe, a graceful deer —
> may her breasts satisfy you always,
> may you ever be captivated by her love.

The Hebrew word for "captivated" is *tishgeh;* it means "to reel, to be intoxicated."[9] The husband is encouraged to reel and to be intoxicated with his wife's love for him.

The Song of Solomon also reveals this love of delight and joy that husband and wife share in their marriage. In 2:4 the bride sees her bridegroom's love as a banner over her. In 2:5 and 5:8 the bride says she is faint with love, or lovesick, as one overwhelmed by his love for her or the greatness of love she feels for him. In 1:8,15,16; 2:14; 4:1-7; 5:10-16; 7:1-9 the bride and bridegroom express how pleased they are with, and how much they appreciate, one another's beautiful physical form and appearance. In 7:1-6, for example, the bridegroom says of his bride, "How beautiful your sandaled feet. . . . Your graceful legs. . . . Your navel. . . . Your waist. . . . Your breasts. . . . Your neck. . . . Your eyes. . . . Your nose. . . . Your head. . . . Your hair. . . . How beautiful you are and how pleasing, O love, with your delights!" In 4:10 the bridegroom expresses how delighted and pleased he is with his bride's sexual love, for the Hebrew word *dod* in the passage refers to the love between the sexes and sexual love. "How delightful is your love, my sister, my bride! How much more pleasing is your love than wine." In 6:9 the bridegroom rejoices in the uniqueness of his wife, who is one of a kind and perfect. "But my dove, my perfect one, is unique."

From the preceding passages we learn another type of love God intended for you to share in your marriage is that you delight and rejoice in one another, that you be intoxicated and captivated with each other's love.

This love of delight in your mate has been referred to as "romance" over the ages. I am reluctant to use the word "romance" to describe this type of love in marriage. I prefer love as a sense of "delight" in one's mate for several reasons. First, "delight" is the manner in which God describes this loving relationship in marriage. Second, "delight" maintains the proper emphasis of what this type of love in marriage is like. This love is not being in love with love, nor enthralled with an emotional situation or atmosphere, nor is it a mystical emotion that is difficult to define and explain. Third, "delight" does not confuse this God-pleasing love in marriage with the sinful lust and desire to possess what is not one's to possess. Such emotions and thoughts are often associated with the word "romance."

My aim is to present love in marriage in the terms God has used for it, not in the terms sinful mankind has used for it. "Romance" is associated with a mixture of emotions from the rapture we also find in the biblical description of "delight" to the sensual lust and desire to possess what is not a sinful man's or woman's right to possess and to an emotionally stirring environment and atmosphere. But there is not a single word for love that I am aware of in either the Old or the New Testament — and used in connection with a God-pleasing marital relationship — which conveys that mixture of emotions associated with the word "romance."

If we look at the different words used for love in the Bible, you will be able to understand what I am saying about the word "romance." The Greek *agape* is a spiritual concern and care that gives and does what is best for the other person.

Its Hebrew equivalent *'āhabh* conveys that meaning as well. In some forms it is used of a loving friend not necessarily of the opposite sex, or of lovers engaged in licentious intercourse, or as a wife who is a lovely delight to behold, as we saw in Proverbs 5:19 above. In fact, the basic meaning of *'āhabh* is "to desire, to breathe after;"[10] it means "to delight in," and it can also denote such feelings as affection and intimacy. The Greek *phileo,* as we have already seen, denotes the warm affection of friends and companions. The Hebrew *dōd* is a love between the sexes, sexual love, or a term for a beloved uncle. *Āhabh* is sinful lust, which appears in connection with adulterous, sexual love. *Rāḥam* denotes tender mercy and compassion, such as God has for us sinners. And *ḥesedh* is a covenant love of loyalty, mercy, and loving-kindness with us sinners, which God has made known in the gospel of Jesus Christ. None of these words fits the definition of "romance" as it is commonly understood today.

"Romance" has been recognized as the equivalent for the Greek word *eros,* from which the word "erotic" is derived. The word *eros* is not used in the Greek New Testament at all. What is more, *eros* in one of its forms or cognates has very limited usage in the Greek translation of the Old Testament, the Septuagint. In the Septuagint this is what we find: In Esther 2:17 it denotes an attraction King Xerxes felt for Esther. In Proverbs 4:6 it denotes a love for wisdom, which is personified as a woman. For the most part *eros* is used for the lovers of an unfaithful, adulterous wife, as in Ezekiel 16:33; Hosea 2:5; and in Ezekiel 23:5,9,30, where it is rendered as the equivalent of the Hebrew ʻāgabh which denotes sinful lust in connection with fornication.

Eros, the equivalent of "romance," is conspicuous by its absence in the Greek Old and New Testaments. If *eros* denoted a God-pleasing love in marriage, one would surely expect to find it in the Song of Solomon, which depicts the love of a bride and groom for one another. But having looked through that book of the Bible in the Greek Septuagint, I am not aware that it is used there.

R. C. Trench in his book, *Synonyms of the New Testament,* wrote regarding the absence of *eros* and its cognates in the Greek Scriptures:

> Their absence is significant. It is in part no doubt to be explained from the fact that, by the corrupt use of the world, they had become so steeped in sensual passion, carried such an atmosphere of unholiness about them . . . that the truth of God abstained from defiling contact with them; yea, devised a new word rather than betake itself to one of these."[11]

Trench noted that *eros* was used also for a yearning desire, and a longing after the unpossessed.

Since *eros,* then, is used in the Greek Old Testament to denote primarily sinful lust in connection with fornication, since *eros* is a word steeped in corrupt, unholy, sensual passion, since *eros* is conspicuously absent in the Scriptures for describing a God-pleasing love, and since "romance" is recognized as the English equivalent for *eros* — "romance" is hardly a fitting term to use for love

136

in marriage as God designed it and pictures it in the Bible.

Furthermore, "romance" is less than a satisfactory word to describe the God-pleasing delight and joy in one's mate because of its meaning in the English language. According to Webster's unabridged dictionary,[12] the noun "romance" was originally a long narrative in one of the Romance languages about the adventures of the knights and other chivalric heroes. Second, it is then used of a fictitious tale which does not deal with everyday life, but with extraordinary and extravagant adventures or mysterious events. It is also used for novels and stories of love, adventure, and exciting real happenings. Then it conveys the excitement, love, and adventure found in such stories or derived from such adventures. In the end it comes to mean an exaggeration or falsehood, and finally a love affair. As a verb, "romance" means to tell or write romantic stories, to be fanciful or imaginative in thinking or talking, and then to make love, court, or woo.

The word "romance," besides its tainted connection with *eros,* simply does not convey what the Lord describes as the love of delight in a God-pleasing marriage. "Romance" makes the emphasis of love an exciting, exaggerated adventure, event, and situation of courting and wooing and making love to, which may even be a purely imaginative, fanciful falsehood. But the correct emphasis of the love that God describes in marriage is a joy and delight and captivation with one's mate which is real and honest.

Following the scriptural picture of love as a delight in one's mate, it is your mate who makes the time you spend together in a given circumstance special, pleasant, and captivating. A candlelight dinner by yourself is neither a joy nor a pleasant experience, nor is it "romantic" in the above worldly sense of the word. Your mate is what makes the difference — not the atmosphere. He or she is what arouses the delight of the moment in the candlelight.

Love as Sexual Desire and a Sexual Relationship

From the beginning God intended that a husband and wife would enjoy sexual love together. That is evident already with Adam and Eve in two ways. First, after God had brought them together in marriage, he said that a husband and wife will be united and become one flesh (cf. Genesis 2:24). That term "one flesh" in the Bible refers to sexual love and intercourse, for 1 Corinthians 6:16 states, "Do you not know that he who unites himself with a prostitute is one with her in body? For it is said, 'The two will become one flesh.' "

Second, it is clear God wanted a husband and wife to share a sexual love in their marriage when he blessed Adam and Eve and instructed them to be fruitful and multiply. There was but one way for them to fulfill that will of God for them and to have children — that was to have sexual intercourse. So when the Lord told them to be fruitful and multiply, he was at the same time telling them to consummate their love for each other in sexual intercourse.

Throughout the Scriptures the Lord upholds sexual love as one type of love in marriage. We saw that in Proverbs 5:18,19. It is also upheld in the Song of Solomon. The bride says in 1:2, "Let him kiss me with the kisses of his mouth — for your love is more delightful than wine." The Hebrew word for love in this passage is $d\bar{o}d$, which denotes a love between the sexes and sexual love. In 4:10 we find this same Hebrew word for sexual love. After delighting in the physical beauty of his wife, the bridegroom says," How delightful is your love, my sister, my bride! How much more pleasing is your love than wine." We find this same word for sexual love in 7:12. Beginning at verse 10 the bride says,

> I belong to my lover, and his desire is for me.
> Come, my lover, let us go to the countryside,
> let us spend the night in the villages.
> Let us go early to the vineyards to see if the
> vines have budded, if their blossoms have
> opened, and if the pomegranates are in
> bloom — there I will give you my *love*.

In 8:3 she then says, "His left arm is under my head and his right arm embraces me."

Jesus upheld the sexual love in marriage when he quoted Genesis 2:24 and said, "The two will become one flesh" (Matthew 19:5). Likewise the Holy Spirit upheld the sexual love in marriage when he quoted that same passage in Ephesians 5:31. We even find in 1 Corinthians 7:3,4 the Lord's instructions that husband and wife are to satisfy each other sexually.

From the preceding passages we learn that another type of love the Lord intended for you in your marriage is sexual desire for your partner and a mutually fulfilling sexual relationship in which the deepest feelings of your love for one another can be expressed.

Love as a Spiritual Concern and Commitment to Do What Is Best for One's Mate

Adam and Eve were both created in the image of God, holy and without sin. In that original state they both loved with a perfect love that was genuinely concerned and committed to giving and doing what was best for the other.

That is the love Scripture says belongs to God and his Christian people. That is the love God commands all people to have for him and for their neighbor — and yes, their spouse too. That is the love which shows itself by doing what is right for God and neighbor through obedience to the commandments. That is the spiritual love encouraged throughout this book, and it is not an emotional love.

This love is seen in the marital relationship in various passages and portions of the Bible. In Ephesians 5:25 husbands are told to have this love for their wives. In Ezekiel 16:1-14 we find this love depicted in the allegory of God taking the Jewish nation as his wife. He took her in when no one else wanted her and everyone despised her. He cared for her, washed her and dressed her beautifully. He did everything that was best for her. This may well be the type of love a wife is displaying when she carries out the Lord's instruction to be a good homemaker who is subject to her husband (cf. Titus 2:5).

This spiritual love of concern and caring is the bedrock of marriage. For in the Song of Solomon 8:6,7 the bride says,

> *Love* is as strong as death, its jealousy (or ardor)
> unyielding as the grave. It burns like a blazing
> fire, like a mighty flame. Many waters cannot
> quench *love;* rivers cannot wash it away.

The two words for love are forms of the Hebrew *'āhabh,* and they are *agape* in the Greek Septuagint. Waters and rivers of water are poetical references to troublesome, hard times. But according to the bride this love is so strong and lasting it cannot be extinguished or washed away by those troubled times.

This spiritual love of concern and commitment, then, will carry you and your spouse through thick and thin, through the good and bad times of your married life. This love will carry you through marital problems when they arise. It will keep you together in difficult times of your life, and it will do what the other types of emotional love we have seen in marriage cannot do.

Why will this love do what the other kinds of love in marriage cannot do? This love lasts. It does not fluctuate as the other emotional loves do. This unselfish, God-oriented and mate-oriented love always moves you to do what is right and what is also good for each other. It always moves you to give generously of yourself and what you have. It loves without regard for what your mate will or can give you in return. It loves, not because your partner is always so lovable, but because it causes you to be such a great lover. This love is exemplified in Proverbs 18:24. There the one who bears this love is described in the NIV as a "friend": "There is a friend [lover] who sticks closer than a brother." He is always there when you need him.

So the last type of love necessary for you to have a happy, satisfying marital relationship is this spiritual love. This is a fruit of the Spirit (Galatians 5:22) that will love in the ways depicted in 1 Corinthians 13:4-7 and according to God's commandments. This love will make your marriage the committed relationship and the pleasantly righteous relationship God made marriage to be from the beginning. This love will be the bedrock of your marriage, and it will keep you together. It will contribute greatly to deepening the love in your marriage.

Marriage is the unique relationship in which all the types of love we have observed may be present in a God-pleasing manner. Those different types of love can and do exist separately, or some of them exist together, in other relationships. But nowhere are all of these types of love so abundantly present in a God-pleasing manner as in the **Christian** marriage.

Endnotes

1. Hebrew $r\bar{e}\,'\bar{\imath}$; Samuel Prideaux Tregelles, translator of *Gesenius' Hebrew and Chaldee Lexicon to the Old Testament Scriptures,* (Grand Rapids, Michigan: Wm. B. Eerdmans Publishing Company, 1971), p 772.

2. Hebrew $ra'y\bar{a}\,th\bar{\imath}$; *Ibid.,* p 774.

3. F. Wilbur Gingrich, *Shorter Lexicon of the Greek New Testament,* (Chicago and London: The University of Chicago Press,1973), p 17.

4. Joseph Henry Thayer, *Greek-English Lexicon of the New Testament,* (Grand Rapids, Michigan: Zondervan Publishing House, 1975) p 653.

5. Gingrich: p 230.

6. *Ibid.,* p 230.

7. Tregelles: p 530.

8. *Ibid.,* p 185.

9. *Ibid.,* p 804.

10. *Ibid.,* pp 15,16.

11. Richard C. Trench, *Synonyms of the New Testament,* (Grand Rapids, Michigan: Wm. B. Eerdmans Publishing Company, 1973), p 43.

12. Webster's *New Twentieth Century Dictionary, Unabridged, Second Edition,* (New York: Prentice Hall Press, 1983), p 1572.

9.

AROUSING, RESTORING, MAINTAINING, AND PROMOTING UNITY AND LOVE

Love in marriage is like a house plant:
When it is nurtured, it thrives;
When it is neglected, it dies.

The evidence that love deteriorates and dies in many marriages is all too plain. Approximately fifty percent of all couples end up filing for divorce. An additional six percent of all marriages have been estimated to fail as well, even though those couples do not file for divorce. Fifty-six percent of all marriages, then, end in failure. What happened to the love those couples shared when they were married? It deteriorated, it died.

Together with your spouse or fiance(e), you need to nurture the love in your relationship. Otherwise you also could lose the love you share.

The purpose of this chapter is to provide information that will assist you in deepening the love in your marriage. And if you are among those who have already lost the love in their marriage, this chapter will discuss what you may do under God to restore it.

The Unity Love Brings into a Marriage

Couples frequently include in their marriage ceremony the lighting of a unity, or wedding, candle. The joining of their two, separate flames into the single flame of the wedding candle symbolizes they have ceased to be two and have become one. The lighting of that candle symbolizes what our Lord Jesus said about marriage: " 'For this reason a man will leave his father and mother and be united to his wife, and the two will become one flesh.' So they are no longer two, but one" (Matthew 19:5,6).

Marriage is a unity. Your marriage vows establish you as a single unit before God. Whether you share the kinds of love described in the previous chapter or not is immaterial to your being one before him. Even in a pretense marriage, in which there is no emotional connection between the man and woman, the two have become one in the eyes of God. By faith in our Lord's word, "They are no longer two, but one," we recognize that unity has come into existence through our marriage vows.

Couples experiencing marital problems, however, do not feel or see themselves as being one, even though they remain so in the eyes of God. They have lost the sense of oneness they once shared. What once caused them to feel and see themselves as one was their love for one another. Love was their unifier. But when that love between them died, they ceased to feel that they were still one.

Love is our unifier. It has from our perspective united us as married couples. Love progressively deepened our relationship and made it more and more meaningful and fulfilling. Love bound us together until we could not bear to be apart.

The Christian couple who possess all the different kinds of love see themselves as one — emotionally, mentally, spiritually, and physically. They are close friends and companions. As such they enjoy the intimacy and the openness, the affection and the trust which exist between them. They know they belong together and only to one another for life. They delight in each other. They feel the excitement and emotion ebb and flow through their relationship. They desire one another and unite sexually, experiencing the pleasurable fulfillment which each gives to the other. They share the same Lord, the same faith, the same goals, the same moral values. They know they are committed with all their hearts to care for and to do what is right for one another. Through those kinds of love, they feel as one in every way humanly possible.

But couples of troubled marriages are not so unified. For the most part, those above kinds of love are missing in their marriage. Their love has deteriorated in proportion to the seriousness of their marital problems and the length of time those problems have existed.

When couples come in for marital counseling, I check whether they still share those different kinds of love. I have found that couples with serious, long-standing marital problems do not feel they are friends and companions, or that they belong together. They do not feel comfortable with one another. Consequently, they do not communicate about intimate matters and personal feelings. They do not delight in one another. They do not make love sexually, and if they do, the experience is sporadic and tense. They do not concentrate on a spiritual love but on their own self-interests.

Such couples are alienated individuals, who admit they are living unhappily and unsatisfactorily in an unfulfilling relationship. They are emotionally disconnected. In extreme cases, they feel numb in their relationship and do not recognize the resentment they feel toward one another. From their vantage point, they are not one, they are two again. The loss of their love for one another destroyed the sense of unity they once shared.

Do you want to enjoy the blessed unity of marriage? Then nurture the feelings of love in your relationship, for those feelings bind you together.

Arousing the Response of Love in a Marriage

In the previous chapters we saw the problems that destroy love and unity in a marriage. Now we want to consider what you and your partner can do to cause love to flourish in your marriage. To begin, let us understand that your emotions as husband and wife are largely a response to what your mate is, says, and does.

A wife once complained to me that her husband did not love her. While her husband did have his personal problems, she seemed a rather cold person who gave her husband little to respond to with warm affection. If she had been a warm, affectionate wife, he may have been a more loving, affectionate husband. The old adage, "What goes around comes around," expresses some truth about love in marriage too.

The Bible reveals that emotions are aroused by what someone else is, says, or does. "A gentle answer turns away wrath, but a harsh word stirs up anger" (Proverbs 15:1). Anger is prevented or stirred up by what another person says and how he says it. "A cheerful look brings joy to the heart, and good news gives health to the bones" (Proverbs 15:30). Joy and happiness are aroused by another person's cheerful appearance and good news. "Do not lust in your heart after her beauty or let her captivate you with her eyes" (Proverbs 6:25). Sinful desires may be stirred up in a man by the beauty of a harlot's form and eyes. In the Song of Solomon we noted the bride and groom stirred up a sense of delight in each other by what they were to each other and by their attractiveness. These passages make it clear that a person's emotions are often a response to what another person is, says, or does.

Psychologists recognize that emotions are aroused by what an individual perceives in his environment,[1] including the other people around him.

From the emotion aroused in a given situation, a certain kind of behavior may result. Fear may cause a person to run away. Anger may lead to retaliation or the correction of an abuse. The emotional experience of feeling loved may motivate a person to show love and kindness in return.

Since the feeling of love can be an emotional response to what each of you perceive in and about your mate, each of you must do what you can to arouse the feeling of love in the other. Each of you needs to give the other all the positive stimuli possible to respond to positively. Each of you needs to be the kind of mate your partner can warm up to and respond to. Receiving warm feelings of love and affection from your partner is dependent to an extent on your giving those warm feelings.

The Restoration of Love in a Marriage

For the sake of you couples who have already lost the feelings of love in your marriage, let us see how you may be able with God's help to restore that love. That same advice will give the rest of us an insight into how we can maintain and promote love in our marriage.

Time and Patience

Over a period of months the feelings of love and affection can be restored to your marriage, but that restoration is often a difficult, step-by-step process. The reasons for that are as follows: First, even with marital counseling you may take two steps forward in your relationship, but then fall back one when an old problem arises again. It then must be addressed and corrected once again.

Second, your mate is hard to win over again after you have hurt and offended him in the past, for he may be unwilling or reluctant to step back into the relationship. "An offended brother is more unyielding than a fortified city, and disputes are like the barred gates of a citadel" (Proverbs 18:19). Therefore, winning your mate over once again can be difficult and time-consuming.

Third, your sinful natures and self-interests responsible for your marital problems must be replaced with new spiritual natures of righteousness and the virtuous fruits of the Spirit, that is, repentance and growth in godly living. Only the Holy Spirit can bring that about in each of you, and he does it only through the power of his word. Such growth in sanctified living is a process that may take some time and should continue throughout our earthly life.

Fourth, you may need to unlearn some bad habits and overcome some lifelong personality problems. That, too, will take some time.

Therefore, while you may be able to restore the love to your marriage with God's help, do not expect this to happen quickly. Remember, the love in your marriage was probably destroyed over a period of years, so it is not going to be restored overnight.

Two Committed Partners

Restoring love to a marriage is not possible in every case. Speaking from a strictly human point of view and not taking into consideration the regenerative power of the Holy Spirit through the gospel, whether or not you restore the feelings of love in your marriage will depend upon you as a couple.

For one thing, the road to a loving marital relationship requires two partners who are willing to take the walk on that road. Are both of you willing to make the effort and to expend the time it will take? If either you or your partner are not committed to mending your marital problems and restoring your marital relationship, you are not likely to do so. The following possibilities could make restoring love to your marriage impossible:

- One of you may decide to obtain a scriptural divorce.
- One of you, being so tired of the hurt and bearing so much resentment, may refuse to try to restore your relationship.
- One of you, thinking you will be unable to restore your marriage even with the help of marital counseling, may be unwilling to try counseling or to make any other sincere effort to save your marriage.
- One of you, being hardened in the sins which destroyed the love in your marriage, may refuse to repent of those faults.
- One of you may blame your spouse for all of your marital problems and insist he or she must make all of the changes, while both of you probably have faults you need to correct in order to save and to improve your marriage.
- One of you may be involved with a third party and be unwilling to break off that adulterous relationship to restore the love to your marriage.
- Both of you may be committed to staying married, but only you yourself are committed to restoring the love to your relationship.

If that last possibility describes your situation, what can you do about it? Your partner's lack of interest in restoring the love to your marriage may stem from an intense resentment toward you over things which happened in the past. His resentment is sinful, of course. He needs to repent, something only God can bring about. But with God's help you can do the following in the hope it will bring your spouse back into your marriage:

- You can be the Christian husband or wife the Lord wants you to be.
- You can put into practice the fruits of the Spirit and the spiritual love to consistently do what is for the good of your spouse.
- You can strive to overcome his evil resentment with good. In the process you may stir up burning coals in his conscience.

If that works, he may start to ask himself why he continues to hold such resentment against you, when you love him so much and do so many wonderful things for him (Romans 12:17-21). Your love and kindness in time may win him over.

Restoring the feelings of love to your marriage, then, depends largely upon the commitment and effort of both of you. If by the grace of God you both are committed to God and your marriage, if you are willing to work at your relationship and at overcoming your own faults that have led to the deterioration of your marriage — then you could succeed in restoring the feelings of love between you.

Reconciliation and Friendship

Granting that each of you has the necessary commitment, how do you begin to restore love to your marriage? This is the key: become true friends again, as you were at the beginning of your relationship. To become friends again means to be reconciled.

The past things you have done in your marriage which hurt one another, made one another's life miserable, and in time destroyed your love for one another, were sins against the Fifth Commandment, "You shall not murder."

Since such sins destroyed the love in your marriage, you need to begin practicing by faith the requirements of the Fifth Commandment to restore that love to your marriage.

Read the following statements of what the Fifth Commandment forbids and demands. As you read these statements, consider what unloving things you and your spouse may have said and done in the past. You may then be able to see your sins against the Fifth Commandment and to understand what you need to correct in your marriage.

> God forbids all words or deeds which harm another person's body, shorten his life, or make his life miserable.
>
> God forbids every hateful thought or word.
>
> God wants us to be patient, kind, and forgiving from our heart toward everyone.
>
> God wants us to help and be a friend to everyone in every bodily need.[2]

Were you able to see the hurtful things each of you has said and done to the other contrary to the Fifth Commandment? Those are the things you need to repent of with the assistance of the Holy Spirit to glorify God in your marriage and to restore your love for one another.

In his sermon on the Fifth Commandment Jesus said,

> Therefore, if you are offering your gift at the altar and there remember that your brother has something against you, leave your gift there in front of the altar. First go and *be reconciled* to your brother; then come and offer your gift. Settle matters quickly with your adversary.

I said above that to restore your love for one another you must be reconciled and become true friends again, instead of remaining the adversaries you are now. Jesus says you are to do that as quickly as possible.

Jesus' words "be reconciled" are the Greek word *diallagethi*. Its basic meaning is "to change the mind of anyone, to reconcile." In Jesus' sermon it means "to be reconciled, to renew friendship with one."[3]

Jesus' words "settle matters" are the Greek word *eu-*

noon. It means "be well disposed to, make friends with."[4] The NASB translates Jesus' statement, "Make friends quickly with your opponent."

Jesus tells you to become well disposed to one another and make friends quickly. Settle those hurtful things which have come between you. In the process, change your spouse's mind about yourself. Exchange your feelings of enmity for a renewed feeling of friendship. When you do, your former feelings of love can return.

Likewise, the apostle Paul says, to be reconciled:

> To the married I give this command (not I, but the Lord): A wife must not separate from her husband. But if she does, she must remain unmarried or else *be reconciled* to her husband. And a husband must not divorce his wife (1 Corinthians 7:10,11).

A wife and a husband have but two options. They may separate from their spouse, but they must remain unmarried and lead a chaste, celibate life; or they can be reconciled to their spouse. Since the Lord has said he does not want a husband and wife to separate, reconciliation is the option to be pursued — either in time after a separation or right away.

The words "be reconciled" in verse 11 are the Greek word *katallageto*. It basically means "to change or exchange." Here it means "to return into favor with someone; to cease to be angry with someone else and receive him back into favor."[5] In this verse the wife is to get back together with her husband. She is to cease being angry with him and receive him back into her favor. She is to return to a peaceful, harmonious relationship with him.

That is what you and your spouse need to do to restore the feelings of love between you. Each of you needs to cease being angry with the other and return to the other's good favor. You need to replace your resentment and alienation with sincere favor and friendship.

But how can you become reconciled and be good friends again? Jesus explains how in Matthew 5:23-25 above. According to Jesus the guilty party is to go and reconcile himself with the person he has wronged and become friends with him again as quickly as possible. Similarly, in Matthew 18:15 Jesus says the innocent party is to go and talk to the person who has sinned against him to win him over.

Now let us apply Jesus' instructions to your marital situation. As an alienated couple, you can achieve reconciliation and renewed friendship in the following manner:

- Confess to one another your past faults and the sins you have committed against each other.
- Be willing to listen to the hurt you have caused the other to suffer.
- Apologize for the wrong you have done and for the hurt you have caused one another.
- Assure one another that you sincerely intend, with God's help, to amend your sinful ways.

When your partner has made that confession, apology, and promise, put away the resentment you had been feeling by forgiving him from the heart (Ephesians 4:31,32). You will no longer hold his past sin against him. You will not keep a record of it in your mind (1 Corinthians 13:5). You will never bring it up to him again. That reconciles each of you to the other. Both of you cease to feel resentment toward one another, and you begin to feel like true friends again. You no longer have any ill feelings between you — only the warm, kind feelings of friendship. You are free to forget about what happened in the past and to resume your former good relationship.

When the two of you have become reconciled, the door is open for the love you felt when you were married to come back into your relationship. You loved one another before, and you are still the same people. You should be able to feel love for one another again, once those past sins and resentments are taken out of the way through reconciliation. Remember this about love and resentment in your relationship:

Love vanishes where resentment lingers,
But forgiveness makes bitterness disappear.

When you were a child, did you have a few special

friends among the children in your neighborhood? I re-member that once in a while one of my friends and I would have some kind of spat. We would get steaming mad at one another, and each of us would stomp home. We did not care if we ever saw one another again. But later we rather tensely and nervously approached one another. We each said we were sorry for what we had said and done, and then we forgave each other. Having done that, we started playing together again. Our renewed friendship felt a little strained at first, but within a few minutes we were having fun and we completely forgot about what had happened between us. In no time we were just as good as friends as we had been before, and we went on in our friendship from there. That is what you want to do in your marital relationship through the process of reconciliation.

Good Deeds and Acts of Kindness

Furthermore, to restore love to your marriage, you need to replace your past sins with good deeds and acts of kind-ness, for emotions follow actions. Your emotions are largely a response to what you are to each other. So be the kind of a person who evokes feelings of love in your part-ner through your good and right words and deeds.

In a troubled marriage the couple needs to overcome the evil that each has been doing to the other. Too fre-quently they repay evil for evil, and this only stirs up more strife and resentment. To overcome the evil that is done to you by your spouse, follow this instruction of the Lord:

> "If your enemy is hungry, feed him; if he is thirsty, give him something to drink. In doing this, you will heap burning coals on his head." Do not be overcome by evil, but overcome evil with good (Romans 12:20,21).

Overcome the distasteful things your spouse has been doing to you by doing good to him. The good you return to him may get through to his conscience like burning coals and make him ashamed of the way he has been acting. Then he will not be likely to repeat his offensive behavior.

Good deeds can also contribute to the restoration of

love in your marriage. The feeling of love in one spouse is often a response to what the other spouse says and does. So those good deeds both of you do for one another give both of you something to respond to favorably — with appreciation and love.

When you are so busy doing good to each other, you will not be committing those past sins against each other, which ruined the love in your marriage. Those love-destroying sins are being replaced with good deeds, which stir up appreciation and favor. Ephesians 4:31,32 tells you to get rid of those bitter feelings you have harbored in the past by being kind, compassionate, and forgiving.

Martin Luther stated in connection with the preceding Romans 12:20,21 passage, "God converts those whom he does convert by showing them goodness. It is only in this way that we can convert a person, namely, by showing him kindness and love."[6] So to convert and win each other over to the side of love and affection and friendship, you each must be kind and loving yourselves.

Spiritual Love and the Power of God's Word

Throughout this book I have emphasized the need to grow in spiritual love by the power of God's word. That need is essential for doing the preceding things to restore love to your marriage as well. The spiritual love God's word arouses in you can contribute to the arousal of the emotional kinds of love you have lost. For that spiritual love will move you to do what is best for your partner, even though he or she has sinned against you in the past. In passages like 1 Corinthians 13:4-7 and Philippians 2:3,4 we have seen what that love can do in one's life and marital relationship.

Furthermore, the law in God's word can do this for you: on the one hand, it can curb your sinful natures from doing the sinful things that have destroyed the love in your marriage; on the other hand, it can guide you as Christians in doing what is right for each other to build up the love in your marriage. We saw, for example, how the law of God can do those two things in your marriage when we looked into the meaning of the Fifth Commandment above.

The Eighth Commandment can also guide you in restoring love to your marriage. In troubled marriages the partners tend to concentrate their attention on the faults of each other. You may have been doing that as well. But the Eighth Commandment says to think positively about one another and to put the best construction on what your mate says and does. "God wants us to take the words and actions of others in the kindest possible way."[7] In 1 Corinthians 13:7 our Lord says that spiritual love believes all things and hopes all things. Using that as your guide, when the two of you have become reconciled, continue to believe and hope your spouse says and does things with the best of intentions, not the worst.

You would do well to follow the instruction of these passages: "Finally, brothers, whatever is true, whatever is noble, whatever is right, whatever is pure, whatever is lovely, whatever is admirable — if anything is excellent or praiseworthy — think about such things" (Philippians 4:8). "Give thanks in all circumstances, for this is God's will for you in Christ Jesus" (1 Thessalonians 5:18). Instead of concentrating on one another's negative points, think about the noble, right, pure, lovely, admirable things in and about each other. Then, thank God for those things you see in each other. When you concentrate on all the favorable traits and virtues you originally saw in one another, the old feelings of love for one another can arise in your hearts once again. And is that not what you want?

The Daily Maintenance and Promotion of Love in a Marriage

Hopefully, those of you who continue to enjoy the love in your marriage were able to observe in the preceding section a number of things that will help you maintain and promote that love. In addition, here are a few things you can do on a daily basis.

Daily reconciliation — Don't let your disagreements and sins against one another remain unsettled and pile up. When disputes or problems arise between you, settle them the same day (cf. Ephesians 4:26,27,31,32; Matthew 5:24,25).

Demonstrate spiritual love daily — Let this love in you do each day what is right and good for each other. Continually display thoughtfulness, kindness, patience, humility, and unselfishness to one another.

Spend enjoyable, meaningful time together — Do things together that you both enjoy. Take or make the time to talk to one another. It is important that you stay closely in touch with one another by sharing your thoughts, feelings, goals, dreams, failures, and disappointments.

Cultivate the comfortable feeling of belonging together and to one another — Be understanding, supportive, and helpful when your partner is going through a difficult time. Be ready to make personal sacrifices for your partner to help him and to be a friend to him. Don't hesitate to tell one another, "I need you." That little statement expresses so much about what your partner means to you and about your desire to remain together.

Delight only in one another — Do not make comments about the attractiveness and desirability of someone else of the opposite sex whom you happen to see. That hurts your partner's feelings, for he wants to be first after God in your heart and life. What is more, when you married your spouse, you promised to forsake all others for him. Also, do not do things which will make your partner feel that he is playing second fiddle to someone or something else. Rather do things that will express your delight in him — dinner alone, flowers, or a card, for example.

Fulfill your partner sexually — This subject will be discussed in detail in the next chapter.

Yes, love in a marriage is like a house plant: When it is nurtured, it thrives; when it is neglected, it dies. I hope this chapter will assist you in preserving and promoting that precious love between you.

Endnotes

1. Jerome Kagan and Ernest Havemann, *Psychology — An Introduction,* (New York, Chicago, San Francisco, Atlanta: Harcourt, Brace & World, Inc., 1968), p 364.

2. David P. Kuske, Board for Parish Education — WELS, Luther's Catechism, (Milwaukee, Wisconsin: Northwestern Publishing House, 1978), pp 88, 89.

3. Joseph Henry Thayer, *Greek-English Lexicon of the New Testament*, (Grand Rapids, Michigan: Zondervan Publishing House, 1975), p 139.

4. F. Wilbur Gingrich, *Shorter Lexicon of the Greek New Testament*, (Chicago and London: The University of Chicago Press, 1973), p 87.

5. Thayer: p 333.

6. Martin Luther, *Commentary on the Epistle to the Romans;* Translation by J. Theodore Mueller (Grand Rapids, Michigan: Kregel Publications, 1977), p 178.

7. Kuske: p 110.

10.

GROWING IN KNOWLEDGE
ABOUT SEXUAL LOVE IN MARRIAGE

As the rising sun dissipates darkness,
So the dawn of knowledge dispels ignorance:
Both bring to light a new world unseen before.

One cannot possibly discuss in seminars or a book how couples can deepen their love without also treating the most intimate part of their relationship — their sexual love. What is more, such information is needed, for biblically sound information on sexual love in marriage is limited. For those reasons I have included this chapter.

God's Word on Sexual Love in Marriage

Scripture is the only place for Christians to begin a discussion on sexual love in marriage. Scripture enlightens us with the truth and dispels misconceptions and false inhibitions. Such biblical information brings to light the sexual happiness with which the Lord wants to bless us in marriage.

Sexual Love in Marriage Is Pure

"Marriage should be honored by all, and the marriage bed kept pure, for God will judge the adulterer and all the sexually immoral" (Hebrews 13:4). The word "pure" in the

Greek means "undefiled, unsullied, pure;[1] that which is unsoiled."[2] What is pure is the marriage bed. The Greek word for "marriage bed" means primarily a bed or couch for lying on, but it also means cohabitation and sexual intercourse.[3] What a husband and wife do together in the privacy of their marriage bed is undefiled, pure, and not sinful, unlike the sexual relationship of men and women outside of marriage.

This word of God frees your consciences to participate in your sexual lovemaking without feelings of guilt. Do not fear that your sexual love is sinful and debasing, as it was regarded by the Victorians. Neither you nor your mate should feel inhibited about your sexual lovemaking. It is a marital activity you can freely enter into and enjoy with the Lord's approval.

Sexual Love in Marriage Is God's Design and Plan

This fact was discussed in chapter 8.

I once explained to a Christian physician that I thought a doctor who believes God created the bodies of man and woman would be able to see better than anyone else that God designed and planned the sexual love of husband and wife. Such a doctor could see by faith that it was no accident that the male and female sex organs complement each other so perfectly. God made those organs to complement one another so the husband and wife could engage in sexual intercourse and be fruitful. The Christian physician agreed with that opinion.

Sexual Intercourse Is a Natural Relationship for a Husband and Wife According to God's Order of Creation

> Because of this, God gave them over to shameful lusts. Even their *women* exchanged *natural relations* for unnatural ones. In the same way the *men* also abandoned *natural relations with women* and were inflamed with lust for one another. Men committed indecent acts with other men, and received in themselves the due penalty for their perversion (Romans 1:26,27).

158

The wicked practice of homosexuality and lesbianism is an unnatural act of inflamed lust. Such acts are a perversion of God's order of creation and nature. But the sexual relations of a man and a woman are "natural relations." God planned those relations to take place, and he created the male and female bodies to be able to engage in them. The sexual relations of a husband and wife, then, are not degrading, disgusting, indecent acts the woman must bear, as the Victorians held.

The Lord Intends Sexual Love to Continue Within the Confines of Marriage

1 Corinthians 7:2-5 states,

> Since there is so much immorality, each man should have his own wife, and each woman her own husband. The husband should fulfill his marital duty to his wife, and likewise the wife to her husband. The wife's body does not belong to her alone but also to her husband. In the same way, the husband's body does not belong to him alone but also to his wife. Do not deprive each other except by mutual consent and for a time, so that you may devote yourselves to prayer. Then come together again so that Satan will not tempt you because of your lack of self-control.

Since the fall into sin, married love is a deterrent to falling into the sin of fornication, for it enables a couple to live a morally pure sexual life. Both can gratify their sexual desires in their lovemaking together.

Giving sexual love to one's partner is called a marital duty. The Greek word for "fulfill" in the above passage means "to give, pay out, fulfill."[4] The Greek word for "marital duty" means "a duty, an obligation, what is one's due."[5] A literal translation of the Greek is, "Let the husband fulfill his duty to his wife."

Providing sexual love for one's mate is an obligation of each mate to the other. When a man and woman enter into marriage, each gives his body to the other. The wife's body belongs to her husband, and his body belongs to her.

During their marriage both are duty-bound to give their body to one another in sexual love. Neither of them has the right to force abstinence from sexual lovemaking onto the other. Any abstinence must be mutually agreed upon, but then it must be only for a limited time of prayer. The husband and wife are to come together again to prevent their falling into the sin of adultery. Their sexual love is to continue throughout their marriage, or until failing health makes it impossible.

God Intends Couples to Enjoy Their Sexual Lovemaking

In the Song of Solomon 1:2 it is written, "Let him kiss me with the kisses of his mouth — for your love is more delightful than wine." The Hebrew word for "love" means love between the sexes. The bride desires her husband's kisses and finds his sexual love and caresses delightful. In 4:10 the groom also states how delightful his wife's sexual love and caresses are.

In Proverbs 5:15-20, referred to earlier, the husband is to enjoy only the woman he has married. He is to be intoxicated and captivated by his wife's sexual love. The pleasure of embracing only her breasts is to satisfy him. The passage reveals that the embraces known as foreplay are a source of delight to the husband and wife during their sexual love too.

What is more, Proverbs 5:19 implies the husband's seeing his wife's lovely figure and breasts is another pleasure of sexual love in marriage. The visual pleasure of seeing one's mate is not wrong. In the Song of Solomon, chapter 4, the husband says about his wife, "How beautiful you are, my darling! Oh, how beautiful! Your eyes. . . . Your hair. . . . Your teeth. . . . Your lips. . . . Your temples. . . . Your neck. . . . Your two breasts. . . . All beautiful you are, my darling; there is no flaw in you." In chapter 5 the wife says about her husband, "My lover is radiant and ruddy, outstanding among ten thousand. His head. . . . his hair. . . . His eyes. . . . His cheeks. . . . His lips. . . . His arms. . . . His body. . . . His legs. . . . His appearance. . . . His mouth. . . he is altogether lovely. This is my lover, this my friend."

Though 1 Corinthians 7:2-5, quoted above, does not specifically mention the husband and wife experiencing sexual pleasure and satisfaction, it is certainly proper to understand that they both will experience those things. What else could be understood from the statements that having a spouse is a deterrent to sexual immorality, that each spouse is to fulfill his marital duty to his partner, and that the body of each belongs to the other?

Scripture reveals that the visual pleasure of seeing one's mate, the embraces in foreplay, and the sexual act of intercourse are all intended by the Lord to be a source of delight, pleasure, and satisfaction to the married couple. Therefore, you and your mate should not feel inhibited from freely enjoying all phases of your sexual lovemaking.

Medical knowledge confirms that the Lord intended sexual love to be a pleasurable experience. The female clitoris, as I verified with a Christian physician, has no known physical function other than to bring about the woman's sexual arousal and release. Since the Lord created the female body with that organ, it is obvious he intended the woman to experience such sexual pleasure in married love. And according to 1 Corinthians 7:3 above, the husband is as obligated to provide his wife with that pleasure as she is to provide him with pleasure. The Victorian idea that the wife is to endure sexual love in her marriage, not enjoy it, is surely a falsehood.

The Meaningfulness of Sexual Love to a Married Couple

As a couple, you want to deepen the love between you. Nowhere is your love so deeply and intimately expressed as in your sexual love. So let us look at what sexual love means to a husband and wife and what their sexual love expresses to one another. We will discover that:

> What lyrics are to a sweet melody,
> Sexual love is to the marital relationship.

For more information on this subject you might read pages 21-43 of Tim and Beverly LaHaye's book, *The Act of*

Marriage.[6] Many of the points I will bring up they also cover in some depth.

You and Your Mate Express Your Mutual Love in the Most Intimate Manner Possible

Sexual love is the deepest expression of all the other kinds of love you feel for one another. The closeness both of you feel in one another's arms and in your marital union satisfies your need for intimacy. In the tenderest manner possible, your sexual lovemaking expresses the intense affection of friendship you feel for one another.

Your sexual love is the most intimate expression of belonging to one another. You are telling and showing one another in the most intense manner that each of you belongs only to the other and that you have forsaken all others. Your sexual love is a graphic demonstration of the "his and hers" concept, the "I am his and he is mine. . . . I am hers and she is mine" relationship described in the Song of Solomon 2:16 and 6:3.

Your sexual love shows how much you delight in one another, in your partner's loving and fulfilling you, in loving and fulfilling your partner. You are able to delight in the pleasure of seeing one another as no one else in the world can. You are able to delight in each other's embraces, foreplay, then ultimately in the marital union. Finally, you are able to delight in the pleasurable release and the peaceful contentment that follows it.

Your Sexual Love Is the Greatest, Most Pleasurable Human Experience

The Song of Solomon 1:2 and 4:10 reflects this ultimate human pleasure "Your love is more delightful than wine. . . . How much more pleasing is your love than wine." The Hebrew word denotes sexual love. No human experience can compare to the sexual love of a husband and wife — beginning with all the kinds of love we saw each is intimately receiving from the other, to the excitement of all the phases of lovemaking through the sexual release, to the final peaceful, relaxed contentment of the afterglow.

Your Sexual Love Also Joins You in a Spiritual Meaningfulness

First, when each of you understands that your

sexual love is a blessing of God for you, you can enter into it with joy and thankfulness to God. Second, the two of you enter into a spiritual relationship with the Lord when you invite him into your lovemaking to use you to create another human being — if that is his will for you. By faith you enter into God's blessing of lovemaking to share with him the most precious privilege of bringing a child into this world.

Your Sexual Love Heightens Your Feeling of Love and Appreciation for One Another

As a result of the fully satisfying pleasure each of you has given the other, you experience that warm feelings of love and appreciation for your partner well up within you. Those feelings are most keenly felt in the afterglow, but they can linger even into the next day.

Your Sexual Love Satisfies Your Sex Drives

Pleasurable lovemaking may fully satisfy you and your spouse. Afterwards you have the feeling of complete fulfillment. Your desire for sexual love is fully gratified. That feeling can last for a while and deters you from seeking sexual gratification outside of your marriage (cf. 1 Corinthians 7:2 above).

Your Sexual Love Builds up the Husband's Sense of Masculinity and the Wife's Sense of Femininity

Giving and receiving sexual pleasure and fulfillment builds up the husband's sense of manliness. He knows he can successfully love his wife and fulfill her, while receiving sexual pleasure himself. In their sexual love he is able to achieve what is unique to men from the beginning of his arousal to his resulting ejaculation. The knowledge that his wife delights in him as the man he is, that she desires him, that she enjoys and appreciates the sexual love he gives her — makes him feel good as a man. Their fulfilling sexual love actually builds up his self-confidence, which in turn can affect other areas of his life.[7] It is not uncommon, on the other hand, that a husband who is impotent has a low degree of self-confidence and self-respect.[8]

Generally, the goal of a wife is to be pleasing to her husband. That is true not only in cooking and homemaking but also in their lovemaking. If she is unable to please her husband sexually and fulfill him, her self-esteem as a woman suffers. Being able to give and receive sexual pleasure, then, also builds up the wife's sense of womanhood and her purpose in life.[9] That in turn can affect other areas of her life too. The knowledge that her husband believes she is lovely, that he desires her, that he enjoys her sexual love and appreciates her — makes her feel good as a woman. And when her husband during their lovemaking treats her as the object of his love and takes the time to fully arouse her and to bring her to fulfillment, she is made to feel like a whole woman. Her sense of femininity soars.

Your Sexual Love Is Relaxing[10]

During the course of your workday, and in connection with situations that arise at home, stress and tension mount. But your sexual release relaxes your nervous system. It releases the day's stress and tension. It gives you a feeling of peacefulness and relaxation. That feeling can carry over to the next day and help you handle the stress of the new day. You may be more congenial, patient, and understanding than you otherwise would have been.

Problems That Undermine Sexual Love in a Marriage

> As a clear sky marks the presence of good weather,
> So sexual happiness is a sign of a good marriage;
> But what dying embers are to a campfire,
> Sexual unhappiness is to a marital relationship.

A variety of common problems undermines sexual love in marriage. Sometimes those problems exist within the sexual relationship itself and adversely affect other areas of the marriage, or sometimes they exist in other areas of the marriage and adversely affect the sexual relationship. If you and your spouse both realize what those common problems are, you can strive to avoid them or to overcome them and thus to deepen the love between you.

Many wives have never experienced a climactic release; many others do not experience such a release regularly — but their husbands almost always do. That is unfortunate for those wives. The Lord also designed the woman's body to enjoy a climactic release — not just once in a single session of lovemaking but even more than once. The lack of fulfillment for a wife can undermine the sexual love in a marriage.

The wife's desire for sexual love is closely related to the pleasantness of, or the dissatisfaction with, the sexual lovemaking of the past.[11] While a woman does have a sex drive, it is not as strong as a man's, and it fluctuates with her monthly cycle. Much of her desire for sexual love is cultivated through the pleasantness and fulfillment she has experienced in past sessions of lovemaking. The more the wife experiences a sexual release and is sexually fulfilled, the more she desires to participate in lovemaking. But the less pleasant and fulfilling the lovemaking has been for her, the less she desires to participate in it. Therefore, for sexual love in a marriage to be all that God designed it to be, the wife's regular fulfillment is just as important as that of her husband.

Various factors in addition to her monthly cycle may contribute to the wife's lack of sexual desire or fulfillment. For example, something may be weighing on her mind, such as: fear — of pregnancy, of how her husband will treat her, or as a result of some traumatic sexual experience in the past like incest or rape; guilt — due to sexual promiscuity before marriage; resentment — particularly toward her husband, or perhaps toward her father. Fear, guilt, and resentment can turn off her mind to sexual love. Then she will not desire it, nor will she be able to achieve sexual arousal and fulfillment.

Frigidity may account for the wife's lack of desire and undermine a couple's sexual love. I am not using the term "frigid" for orgasmic impairment resulting from a psychological problem.[12] I am using the term for a lack of desire for the sexual relationship,[13] which develops over a period of time during the marriage. The inconsiderateness of her husband can bring about such a lack of interest in sexual love .

A husband's arousal can be almost instantaneous, his release likewise. Sexual desire can burn within him all day long. But his wife is not like that. All day or evening she may not think about making love. She may not feel any desire for sexual love. Her husband then needs to take the time and make the effort to awaken that desire in her. He then needs to arouse and stimulate her sufficiently until she can experience an exciting climactic release.

Unfortunately, not all husbands understand that about their wives. In their ignorance, or in their haste to satisfy themselves, they do not sufficiently arouse and stimulate their wife in pleasurable foreplay. They cut the foreplay short, then blame their wife afterwards for being cold and not achieving a sexual release. But in reality the problem rests with them.

After years of the husband's ignorant or hasty lovemaking, the wife begins to feel used and abused. She comes to feel she is only an object her husband uses to satisfy himself. Too frequently she has felt her husband roll over satisfied to go to sleep — just when she was becoming fully aroused. After years of that, she has no desire for such lovemaking. She has become frigid — not because she was naturally that way but because of her husband's inconsiderateness.

The obvious solution is for the husband to learn that his wife needs more time. If you are a wife who has this problem, explain to your husband what has been happening to you and urge him to take the time for adequate foreplay.

Some wives are left unfulfilled because their husband has a premature ejaculation. His sudden ejaculation is not deliberate. On the contrary, he himself may be depressed by it and wish he could control it. Being unable to satisfy his wife in intercourse may make him feel like a failure and less than a man.

A husband can try to do some things to gain control of his ejaculation. The husband who has this problem should seek out such information from a reliable source and work at gaining his control.[14] His wife's understanding and support will be most beneficial to him in the process.

Selfishness

Sexual love is the most intimate expression of the husband's and wife's love for one another. It therefore is mate-oriented, for both concentrate on giving pleasure to the other. Both unselfishly please one another so their lovemaking becomes a mutually escalating state of arousal that proceeds to the marital union and their ultimate intense release.

But when both of them concentrate on attaining sexual pleasure for themselves, their selfish preoccupation undermines that mutually arousing lovemaking. Their sexual relationship becomes more a relationship of "lovetakers" than "lovemakers." Since neither of them is giving to the other the loving pleasure they otherwise could, they are unable to experience the height of sexual arousal or intense release they otherwise could. Their preoccupation with obtaining pleasure for themselves actually diminishes the pleasure they receive. In sexual love the less one gives, the less one receives.

Misconceptions or Inhibitions

Misconceptions, such as the Victorians had, and inhibitions can prevent a couple from experiencing the fullest possible pleasure in their relationship, for they feel less than free to engage in their sexual lovemaking.

Lack of Knowledge

The husband's ignorance, for example, that his wife needs more time in arousing foreplay prevents them from reaching the highest possible level of sexual pleasure.

A knowledge of the male and female anatomy, of how the various organs of each function, and of how to fulfill one another is imperative. Lacking that knowledge, a couple will be unable to find the most pleasing techniques to arouse one another to full satisfaction .

A husband and wife should also understand that their sex drives are different. The sex drive of the husband is much stronger than that of his wife and remains constant, while his wife's fluctuates with her monthly cycle. Consequently, he wants and requires sexual fulfillment more often than she does. During a marital counseling session one wife said to me about her husband, "He's a sex maniac! All he wants to do is make love! When he comes home from work, at night, Saturday and Sunday afternoons — all he wants to do is go to bed!" Wives such as that one fail to understand that their husbands are healthy males whose bodies are daily producing millions of sperm and seminal fluid, which produce the desire for release. On the other hand, husbands fail to understand that their wife's sex drive does not create the desire for such frequent releases and that much of her drive is cultivated through a history of pleasant sexual experiences with him. What we often see in marriages today, then, is this: wives tend to think their husbands are sex maniacs; husbands tend to think their wives are cool or indifferent toward sex. Each judges the other on the basis of his or her own sex drive. A proper understanding of the male and female sex drives is necessary for marital harmony.

Dr. Ed Wheat's book, *Intended for Pleasure,* can provide you with helpful information on sexual love in marriage. I have some theological differences with his book, but his is the best book from a Christian perspective I have come across on the subject.

Lack of Communication

Unfortunately, some couples do not discuss their sexual lovemaking. When that happens, each is left in the dark to imagine or conclude what he or she will. They need to communicate about their sexual love, just as they need to discuss other areas of their marriage to gain a better understanding of one another. If the husband is going to fulfill his wife, he needs to know what is pleasing and arousing to her and what is not. She likewise requires that kind of information about him. Each of them should feel free to discuss beforehand, and during lovemaking, areas they find pleasingly arousing or areas they do not. Likewise, they can talk about new techniques and agree or disagree on some experimentation. Couples who do not discuss their sexual lovemaking are cheating themselves out of knowledge and pleasure which otherwise could be theirs.

Problems in Other Areas of the Marriage

Sexual love in marriage is like a barometer which reads the highs or the lows in the rest of the relationship. When the rest of the marriage is loving and harmonious, the sexual love is what it should be also. On the other hand, problems in other areas of the marriage make their way into the bedroom too.

> As a barometer falls when a storm
> moves through the land,
> so sexual love declines when tempests
> blow through the marriage.

It can be difficult for the husband, and impossible for the wife, to argue during the day and then fall into one another's arms in passionate desire at night. As one troubled wife once explained to me, "We fight all day long. Then when we go to bed at night my husband expects me to be ready to make love with him. And I can't!"

Couples who have come in for counseling with serious marital problems do not enjoy sexual lovemaking as they once did. Their sexual love has either been discontinued for long periods of time, or their sexual love is very sporadic and infrequent without giving them the fulfillment it once did. Their other marital problems caused their sexual love to break down.

Impotence

Impotence has a variety of causes. Medications for heart trouble, high blood pressure, or mental disorders or medications containing antihistamine can cause impotence. So can diabetes or the abuse of alcohol or drugs

Impotence may develop in middle age. A husband who had no previous trouble making love to his wife may suddenly be unable to ejaculate during intercourse. Such an unexpected failure can then trigger fear within him, for he does not understand that in middle age he may sometimes have such an experience. So his fears and doubts about his manliness grow, and his ability to achieve and maintain an erection in future lovemaking sessions is impaired. Those failures feed his fears and self-doubts, with the result that he may become impotent.[15]

Dr. Ed Wheat has stated that 75% of the impotent men undergoing treatment had some organic condition that could have contributed to their impotence. He also noted, however, that in more than 75% of the men treated these mild to moderate psychological problems were associated with their impotence: inhibition, shame and avoidance, anger and hostility, fear of intimacy, feelings of insecurity or personal inadequacy, or guilt.[16]

I once counseled an impotent husband who had come to me for help with some other problems. He had sought treatment and had undergone a number of medical tests to discover the cause of his impotence He had learned that nothing was physically wrong with him, yet he was impotent. His problem rested in his mind. As one sexologist explained when I brought up this case, "The problem of impotence frequently rests in the most important sexual organ of all — the one between the ears."

Help is available for men who are impotent. The great majority can regain their ability to function fairly well.[17] Tim LaHaye went so far as to say that ninety times out of a hundred impotence can be cured.[18] If you are an impotent husband, you might read and discuss with your wife the material in Dr. Ed Wheat's book,[19] and in Tim and Beverly LaHaye's book.[20] You may also want to consult your physician or other qualified counselor. With such help you may be able to overcome your impotence and enjoy sexual love with your wife once again.

Fatigue

Fatigue can be another contributing cause to impotence, for it can leave a husband or wife without the energy for sexual lovemaking. Rest, sleep, or a vacation from work can clear up this problem.

Fantasizing

Fantasizing takes place when a husband or wife dreams he or she is making love with someone else while making love with one's spouse. This is sinful lust, which constitutes adultery (Matthew 5:28). Christian husbands and wives will want to avoid this sin.

Fantasizing may reveal a dissatisfaction with the body or the sexual love of one's spouse. But that ought not to be. As we learned from Proverbs 5:19, a husband, for example, should be satisfied with the breasts of his wife and be captivated by her love. He ought not to be dreaming about caressing the breasts of another woman and being captivated by her love.

Fantasizing undermines the oneness of the husband and wife by mentally bringing into their sexual relationship a third party who does not belong there. It destroys the sense of belonging together and only to one another, for the fantasizer mentally gives himself to someone else. If the innocent partner should learn that his or her mate was fantasizing about making love to someone else during their lovemaking, he or she may be crushed, and their sexual love may be destroyed because of it.

Foul Language

A husband may make vulgar remarks about his wife's anatomy or about the height of her passion. Shocked and degraded, his wife may find further sexual arousal difficult or impossible. A husband will want to clean up his language for the sake of his Lord as well as for his wife, for such language is a sin against the Sixth Commandment.

Lack of Privacy

A husband and wife need the assurance they will not be overheard or that someone, like one of the children, will not barge in on them. Making love with those fears is difficult and limits the times a couple can make love safely. The best thing a husband and wife with children can do is install a lock on their bedroom door. A radio, stereo, or tape recorder playing music may assure audible privacy as well.

Nothing I am aware of so distorts the image and understanding of God-pleasing married love as does pornography. Pornography inflames the heart and mind with lust, often for sexual excesses that are degrading, debasing, and abusive. Pornography is sin. Ephesians 5:3 states, "Among you there must not be even a hint of sexual immorality, *or of any kind of impurity* . . . because these are improper for God's holy people."

In premarital counseling I explain to young couples that sexual love in marriage is nothing like the imaginative romance, exaggerated desire, or gross sexual behavior they may have seen in movies, magazines, or books. I inform them that, when they learn by experience that their sexual love is not like what they had pictured it would be because of that pornography or those Hollywood love scenes, they could begin to think there must be something wrong with them or their love. I advise them to discard pornography as sin and not be influenced by it.

Contrary to what the pornography industry pictures, a normal woman is not an insatiable nymphomaniac who is always ready to jump into bed on a moment's notice. Nor is she a sexual object for a man to use, abuse, and then discard at will. In marriage the woman is the man's wife — the sensitive, caring, emotional woman God has made for him, who needs his affection, attention, and tenderness. She is God's blessing to him, and he needs to recognize and treat her as such (Proverbs 18:22; 1 Peter 3:7).

Pornography may influence a husband to expect or even demand that his wife engage in sexual practices that are perverted and degrading to her. His mind may become so inflamed with sinful lust and sexual excesses that he believes he must engage in such activities to achieve sexual gratification. If he does insist on them, he may not only hurt his wife and adversely affect their sexual love together; he may diminish the quality of their marriage as a whole — not to mention the peril to his own soul due to pornography.

Furthermore, the sexual lust and excesses of pornography can so inflame a husband's mind that he abandons the sexual love of his wife, because she fails to excite him enough. He may skid down the ladder of sin into masturbation, using pornography or a sexual fetish, such as a woman's bra or panties; or, he may decline into the sexual cesspool of rape, pedophilia, or homosexuality. I well remember the hurt of one wife I counseled: after years of using pornography her husband had abandoned her for the warped excitement of using sexual fetishes to masturbate. I am convinced that pornography is addictive and can result in gross sexual perversions and excesses.

Some General Principles to Maintain and Promote Sexual Love in Your Marriage

Keep Peace and Harmony in Your Marriage

Be reconciled to each other before day's end and do not go to bed angry with one another, as explained in earlier chapters. Remember, you do not feel in love, nor desire to make love, when the two of you are angry and alienated.

Preserve and Promote the Other Types of Love in Your Relationship

We learned in chapter 8 what those loves were.

If you are the husband, you may need to awaken your wife's desire for sexual love. At times your wife may initiate sexual lovemaking. For the most part however, she is chiefly the responder — you are the lover. Your wife may not think about making love during the day or evening. During those hours she needs your attention, affection, kindness, and tenderness to respond to before making love. If you have satisfied those needs of hers, she is more likely to respond favorably to your sexual advances when you initiate lovemaking.

If you are the husband, understand that making love to your wife begins before you go to bed. Spend time beforehand to talk to her about meaningful things regarding your life and marriage. Show her love and affection. Nurture close companionship. Foster the sense of belonging together. Express your delight in her. By doing so you cultivate the emotional attachment and oneness necessary for a meaningful physical oneness. Providing for her emotional needs can at the same time arouse her desire for sexual love.

Be Knowledgeable about Sexual Love

Understand what the Lord says about sexual love in marriage. Then with clear consciences and thankfulness to God the two of you can freely enter into your lovemaking without inhibiting fears and misconceptions. Also, be familiar with the male and female organs and how they function. Then learn how to pleasingly stimulate one another to full arousal and release.

Communicate about Your Sexual Love

If you have had difficulty getting into such a discussion, why don't you read and discuss this chapter together in order to break the ice and provoke discussion? Talk about whatever will build understanding between you and improve your sexual relationship.

Husbands, Be Gentle with Your Wife during Your Lovemaking

Husbands frequently have more strength in their hands and arms than they realize. As a result, when they squeeze or hold their wife, they may unknowingly hurt her. A wife cannot respond warmly and become aroused by what inflicts pain. Every wife wants her husband's warm affection. She senses that true love through his soft, gentle, tender embraces and touches, which arouse her and move her to respond. Physical force and violence may turn on sin-sick masochists or sadists, but it does nothing for a wife except to hurt her and move her to withdraw from her husband's advances.

Each of You, Make It Your Goal to Please and Fulfill Your Partner

Be intent upon giving pleasure to your mate. Husbands and wives can feel a tremendous pleasure from fully arousing and pleasing their mate. One husband explained to me he gains more gratification from pleasuring his wife than he does from receiving pleasure himself. Learn to enjoy that pleasure of pleasing your mate also.

Take the time for adequate, enjoyable foreplay, especially for the wife's sake. Sometimes the two of you may be so aroused at the outset that you both desire sexual intercourse almost at once. But that is probably the exception, not the rule.

Fully and freely give yourself to your mate for his pleasure, for that is what the Lord wants you to do (1 Corinthians 7:3,4). Therefore, do not mentally withhold yourself from your mate. If you are a new bride or young wife, you may have some inhibitions and difficulty doing that. But the word of God makes it clear that sexual love in marriage was designed by the Lord and is pure in his sight, so you may relax in your husband's arms and mentally as well as physically give yourself to him. What is more, your mind needs to be fully involved with and committed to your sexual lovemaking for your own arousal and climactic release.

Take Care of Yourselves Physically

You need energy and good health to enjoy sexual love.

Compliment Your Partner on His or Her Appearance

Do not criticize your partner's physical appearance. Your criticism inflicts deep emotional hurt by attacking your partner at the heart and core of his masculinity or her femininity. Your mate will then find it difficult or impossible to make love with you.

Rather delight in each other. Both of you desire to feel that your mate delights in you. A genuine compliment and word of praise will warm his or her heart and evoke a positive, loving response. It would do you both good to remember that out of all the other men, or women, in the world, the Lord has made this one man or woman just for you. Is that not good reason to rejoice in him or her?

Pay attention to your personal cleanliness and grooming. Before going to bed and making love, a couple will enhance their relationship and one another's arousal if they freshen up with a shower, comb their hair, and apply a little after-shave lotion or perfume. Every wife's dresser drawer could use some negligee to round out her wardrobe, so she can reserve her footed pajamas for cold winter nights when her husband is away on a business trip. Such preliminary pampering and fussing says to your mate, "You are special! And I want to be special for you. I love you and I want to be as pleasing to you as I can be." Then you can relax and enjoy the depths of the love you share for one another.

Endnotes

1. Greek *amiantos;* F. Wilbur Gingrich, *Shorter Lexicon of the Greek New Testament,* (Chicago and London: The University of Chicago Press, 1973), p 10.

2. Joseph Henry Thayer, *Greek-English Lexicon of the New Testament,* (Grand Rapids, Michigan: Zondervan Publishing House, 1975), p 32.

3. Greek *koite; Ibid.,* p 352.

4. Greek *apodidoto;* Gingrich: p 23.

5. Greek *opheilen; Ibid.,* p 157.

6. Tim and Beverly LaHaye, *The Act Of Marriage,* (Grand Rapids, Michigan: Zondervan Publishing House, 1976).

7. *Ibid.,* pp 23,24.

8. *Ibid.,* p 23.

9. *Ibid.,* pp 34-36.

10. *Ibid.,* pp 27,28,29,42.

11. *Ibid.,* p 42.

12. A woman who does have an orgasmic impairment should consult a competent professional counselor or her physician. Following the lead of David Reuben, M.D., such a condition is probably the result of serious emotional deprivation during childhood and after. For more information on orgasmic impairment, or frigidity, the reader could consult Dr. Reuben's book, *Everything you always wanted to know about sex, but were afraid to ask;* Dr. Ed Wheat's book, *Intended for Pleasure;* Tim and Beverly LaHaye's book, *The Act of Marriage.*

13. LaHaye: p 128.

14. A husband experiencing premature ejaculation may benefit

from reading Dr. Ed Wheat's book, *Intended for Pleasure,* pp 89-99; and Tim and Beverly LaHaye's book, *The Act of Marriage,* pp 128-130 and 173-175. If further help is needed, he should discuss his problem with a competent counselor or physician.

15. LaHaye: p 156.

16. Ed Wheat, M.D. and Gaye Wheat, *Intended for Pleasure,* (Old Tappan, New Jersey; Fleming H. Revell Company, 1981 revised edition), p 122.

17. *Ibid.,* p 120.

18. LaHaye: p 157.

19. Wheat: pp 119-129.

20. LaHaye: pp 155-181.

11

KEEPING YOUR MARRIAGE
LIKE A SWEET HONEYMOON

A honeymoon may be like a surprise —
The beginning of even better things to come,
Or the end of the good things that had been.

Too frequently the joke becomes a reality.

When my son, Chris, was about to be married, the men in his office teased him. They joked that they had decided to give him a sympathy card for his wedding present.

Why do men always tease prospective grooms that marriage is a terrible loss of happiness? Why do they make getting married a time to pity the poor groom with expressions of regret and sympathy? How often does the groom hear, "Wait until the honeymoon is over"?

The jokes about how bad marriage is are meant in fun, but I wonder if such jokes started and have continued because for so many husbands and their wives the honeymoon indeed has ended.

For too many couples, the joy, the love, the pleasantness they felt when they were married come to an end. During the years after their honeymoon their marriage slips. They lose the excitement of their relationship, the warmth of their first love, the thrill of their sexual lovemaking, the fun of doing enjoyable things together. To such an unhappily married couple maybe a sympathy card on their anniversary would not be so out of order.

But why should couples come to look back over the years of their marriage and sigh, "What ever happened to the good old days of our honeymoon, when we were young, in love, and happy together?" Marriages need not be like that. They could be so, so much better! Couples can maintain and promote the excitement and pleasantness of their initial married love throughout the years of their marriage — no matter how many years they are married. Their honeymoon could be the beginning of deepening love and intimacy that get better and better for many years to come.

But what can you do to keep your marriage like a sweet honeymoon? Certainly you do not want your marriage to deteriorate to the point that a sympathy card would be appropriate on your anniversary. Let us first observe what kinds of things take the honeymoon out of a marriage. Then you will know what to guard your marriage against. Afterwards, let us note some simple, basic things you can do to keep the honeymoon in your marriage.

When the Honeymoon Fades from a Marriage

Too frequently couples let their hair down after their wedding and honeymoon. As they do, the excitement and joy of their relationship fade.

Couples Lose Their Former Concern for Their Relationship

After the wedding and honeymoon, couples begin to take their relationship for granted. As their indifference grows, their relationship deteriorates. Their appreciation of their partner decreases instead of increasing.

Couples develop the attitude that they can relax in their relationship. They feel they no longer must put forth the effort to allure their mate as they did before. They do seem to realize that their love is largely a response in each of them to what they see in their mate. So they do not continue to be the man or woman they were to arouse emotions in one another. As they proceed to give each other less to respond to, their mutual feelings of love and appreciation dwindle.

For example, the initial concern of the husband during the couple's courtship was to woo and to win the lady so she would love him and want to marry him. But after marriage that concern passes. He begins to give his wife less love and affection to respond to. On the other hand, the initial concern of the wife during the couple's courtship was to be that sweet, charming, alluring woman of her man's dreams so he would want to marry her. But after marriage that concern passes. She begins to give him less love to respond to. As they both become indifferent and lose their initial concern to attract one another, their feelings of mutual attraction decrease, along with their feelings of love and appreciation.

Couples also lose their initial concern to make one another happy. While they were dating, each one tried to be as agreeable as possible and bent over backward to accommodate the other. Each was willing to give in and make compromises for the benefit of the other. Each tried to find out what the other liked and enjoyed doing. Each then did those things with the other, even when he had little interest in doing those things himself.

But that initial concern to please one another often wears off after the wedding. Gradually the man and wife become more independent, more self-centered, and less inclined to do the things they did for one another while they were dating.

For example, the husband has always hated shopping. Now that he is married, he refuses to take his wife shopping as he did while they were courting. She can go by herself. He would rather watch a baseball game. The wife, on the other hand, is bored with baseball. While they were courting, she watched ball games only to please him. Why should she sit out in the heat, get fried to a crisp by the sun, and dry out her skin and her hair, when she is bored to death? She would rather stay home where it is air conditioned.

Consequently, as time goes on, they do fewer things together than they did while they were dating. Both become disgruntled that their partner will not do the things he or she used to do. Each grows to miss the friendship and companionship they shared when they did those things together. Their relationship then suffers, because the former fun and excitement of doing those things together is lost.

Couples Become Careless about Their Habits and Their Manners after Marriage

Couples stop trying to look their best for one another. While they were dating, both took the time to make themselves as attractive as they could for the other. Before a date he showered, shaved till his face bled, generously applied after-shave lotion, and dressed in the most stylish clothes. Meanwhile she spent hours pampering and fussing and dressing most attractively. When she met her man for the evening, she was as radiant as a star and as fragrant as a new spring rose. Then they delighted in each other.

But after their marriage and honeymoon they become careless about their looks and attire. They do not make the effort to be that handsome Prince Charming or that beautiful woman of his dreams. I am not saying that in their daily life and work routine they should always be dressed up to go to a ball. But there are times to fuss and dress up for one another. If there is anyone we want to look our best for, it ought to be our spouse.

That little added grooming for one another, however, fades from the relationship. Permit me to give you a somewhat exaggerated example. Throughout the day the husband works in his office with women who are attractively dressed. They are groomed, manicured, perfumed, and wearing nylons and heels. Meanwhile his wife slaves at home with the housework, washes dirty clothes and dishes, chases after the toddlers from sunup, and cleans up the children's messes one after the other all day long. When he comes home from work, she looks a sight. Her hair is a mess. She has no makeup on. She is wearing sweat pants stained down the front from the baby's breakfast. When he sees her after working with the well-groomed women at the office, he feels let down. If she had taken just a few minutes to change and to groom herself before he came home, she could have made his homecoming a happy one — one he would look forward to again.

Husbands can be careless about themselves too. A husband may lounge around the house in a smelly T-shirt, oil-stained pants, bare feet, and a day's growth of sandpaper on his face. After a while his wife begins to long for the knight in shining armor who had once ridden into her life and had taken her breath away. But his shining armor has become dirty, tarnished, and smelly.

Carelessness about cleanliness and grooming before going to bed may also slip into a marriage. When that happens, a little more of the honeymoon fades from the relationship.

Likewise, carelessness about personal habits and manners causes the honeymoon to slip out of sight. A man or woman who is courteous, respectful, considerate, humble, as well as friendly, is charming and attractive, but people find ill-mannered individuals offensive and undesirable.

That is true also in marriage. At the outset of their relationship the couple put their best manners forward, for each wants to be charming and attractive to the other. Each wants to be a courteous, respectful, considerate person the other will desire to be with. Therefore, each one uses his or her good manners to help cultivate a pleasing relationship.

But after marriage the couple begin to take their relationship for granted. They become unconcerned about using their best manners. They cease striving to be the charming person for their mate they previously had been. As a result, some of the former pleasantness of being with one another fades from their relationship.

Some of these little courtesies also disappear after their marriage: "Thank you;" "You are welcome;" "Excuse me." Those courteous expressions will not make or break a marriage, but they do add a certain charm and pleasantness to a couple's relationship. They do make the husband and the wife more attractive and desirable to one another.

Vulgarity and cursing in God's name surely detract from

the pleasantness of a marital relationship. Furthermore, such language makes the husband and wife unattractive. Any woman who uses such language — no matter how beautiful she may look — makes herself look coarse, hard, ugly. The same is true of a man. Only those who regularly hear and use vulgarity and profanity fail to notice this about themselves or their mate.

Good table manners are as important after marriage as they were before. Before marriage when a couple went out to dinner, they exhibited their best table manners. For (if I might use this gross exaggeration) if the man ate his mashed potatoes with his fingers, the lady would not want to see him again. If the lady chewed with her mouth gaping open so she drooled food down her chin, the man would never want to date her again. If a man and woman are offended by bad table manners before they are married, they will also find such manners offensive after they are married. And bad manners rob their relationship of some of its pleasantness.

The husband who belches loudly after dinner does not appear debonair and charming to his wife. Her impression of him is just the opposite — a slob would be a better description — and she then wonders what ever happened to the charming, well-mannered man she fell in love with.

Couples Put Other Matters before Their Marriage and Being Together

In a mutually pleasing Christian marriage both partners make their marriage second in importance only to God and his kingdom. Because it is pleasing to their Savior-God, they strive by faith to make their marriage what he says it should be. Building such a marriage is an important part of living their Christian life. Therefore, they put their marriage before other things and continue to do things that will make it better and more enjoyable. But when couples do not consciously set such a priority in their marriage, other things can easily get more attention than they deserve.

Some couples put their careers before their marriage. In

the past the husband was usually the one who spent too much of his time and energy on his career. But today more and more women also pursue careers outside the home. They too now expend more and more of their time and energy in their career rather than in their marriage. As a result, many marriages break down and end in divorce. More than one husband has told me after his wife divorced him that he would gladly throw out his career if only he could have his wife back. But it was too late.

Outside hobbies, recreation, or organizations may take too much time from a couple's marriage. When a husband or wife begins to substitute outside interests for time together, their marital relationship suffers. On the other hand, when a marriage has begun to falter, husbands and wives may substitute outside interests for their marital relationship. In this way they cause their marriage to deteriorate even more.

Watching television can be a hindrance to a marriage. The family's television may do more to undermine a couple's companionship and communication than anything else in the home. Television viewing replaces sitting together to talk and be intimate. What is more, either one of them may sit up to watch the late night programs while their mate goes to bed alone. Thus the television can even interfere with their sexual lovemaking. For these reasons I tease couples in premarital counseling not to purchase a television until they have been married at least several years. They know I am teasing them, but they get the point.

The Husband's Chivalry Fades Back into the Middle Ages

The husband fails to show his wife little courtesies. In the good old days of their courtship he showed his respect for the woman of his life with many courtesies. He opened doors for her. He opened and closed the car door for her. He drove her up to the entrance to let her out, so she would not have to walk through the rain. He helped her put on or take off her coat. He slid her chair in for her at the table in the restaurant. But after they have been married for a while, he forgets to do those things which made her feel special and honored. One more little nicety of the good old days then fades from their relationship.

Couples, Husbands Especially, Become Forgetful

Being wonderful, emotional creatures of God, wives are touched when their husbands remember them on their birthday, wedding anniversary, Christmas, or Valentine's Day. While wives may become forgetful too, during the years of marriage it is usually the husbands who forget to give at least a card on these occasions.

The little surprises that once spiced up the couple's relationship are forgotten after their honeymoon, or perhaps the couple agree not to purchase gifts and cards for one another anymore. Before marriage the surprise gifts or cards were little remembrances of love, which were given for no special reason other than the couple loved one another. But as the days of their marriage pass, so may those little surprises. One more small bit of the honeymoon relationship then disappears.

The dates cease after the honeymoon. During their courtship the young man asked his future wife to dine out with him. He took her to a comfortable restaurant with a pleasant atmosphere. They relaxed and had an enjoyable time. She enjoyed those opportunities to fuss over herself and dress up to be the beautiful woman in his eyes that she wanted to be. When he told her over dinner how lovely she looked, her self-esteem soared and she felt good about herself. But after the wedding the husband gradually stops asking his wife to go out for dinner. As those dinner dates disappear, some more of the luster and glitter of their relationship fades into memory.

Whether the wife is consciously aware of it or not, she may miss those opportunities, such as a dinner date, to be the woman she was and would still like to be, as well as the compliments that lifted her self-esteem and made her feel good. She may also begin to miss being asked for a date by her husband, which would show her he is still interested in her. Being asked for a date would stir up the old memories and some of the thrill she had felt when he asked her out before their marriage.

Some husbands have their secretary order flowers or pick out a gift for their wife. Those husbands depend upon their secretary to do what they should do for themselves. Such a husband fails to realize that his wife wants a gift from her husband, not from her husband's secretary. The thought, the consideration, the time invested in selecting the gift are more meaningful to a wife than the gift itself. In my marriage seminars I have asked the wives whether they would rather have a dozen beautiful roses ordered by their husband's secretary or a handful of dandelions picked by their own husband. They all chose the dandelions!

Tender Expressions of Love and Affection
Dwindle or Cease after the Honeymoon

Before marriage a couple frequently telephoned one another. During those conversations they expressed such feelings as, "I miss you. I love you." They may also have sent one another love letters while they were going together, especially if they were apart for a while, and left love notes for one another to find. When they were alone together, they regularly whispered, "I love you, darling. I need you. I want you."

But after they are married, those telephone calls to say "I love you" cease. Likewise, the notes are seldom or never written. A whole day may pass, two days or more, in extreme cases weeks or months or even years may pass, without them saying to one another, "I love you, dear. You mean the world to me." The love and affection upon which their whole relationship was founded is not expressed as often as necessary to reinforce those feelings in one another. The less their love and affection are expressed, the more they may wonder whether those feelings even exist any longer, the more they may become emotionally disconnected, and the more their honeymoon fades away.

A Couple's Intimate Communication Wanes

When a couple has begun dating, it is not uncommon for them to talk for hours about their likes and dislikes, their goals in life, their past failures, their dreams, their plans, their hopes. After they have fallen in love and the idea of marriage has arisen, they spend hours laying plans for their life together, making their wedding and honeymoon plans, discussing how many children they would like to have, and talking about a host of other subjects important to them. The talks that last until the wee hours of the morning pass quickly, for those hours seem like only minutes to them. They enjoy themselves immensely just talking. Those talks were exciting times of getting to know one another intimately. Those talks were bringing them closer together emotionally. Through those talks they were in touch and in tune with one another.

But after they are married, they learn they have exhausted those subjects which brought them so close together. And the longer they are married, the less they have to talk about, and the rarer those intimate talks become.

What is more, because they do not have intimate talks such as they once had, through the passing years they fail to stay in touch with one another. They do not share the failures or successes they experience and feel, their lingering old dreams or new ones, the plans and goals they still want to achieve in life, or the modified ones they feel compelled to accept. As they mature and their thoughts and feelings change, they do not share with one another what is happening to them. Gradually, then, they lose contact with one another. Years later they feel they do not know one another as they once did. Each has changed, but they have not shared that with one another and changed together. They have become disconnected. Furthermore, they may miss — and this is particularly true of the wife — the many pleasant hours of such intimate conversations, like the talks which first kindled the excitement of their relationship.

Couples Slip into the Boredom of Daily Routine

Before marriage they were continually going places together. They enjoyed interesting times together. But as time goes on after marriage, they become caught up in the daily and weekly routine of work, domestic duties, and raising their children. Their weekends are spent shopping, making house repairs, doing odd jobs. They do not take the time to do things for themselves. For years they may not get away by themselves for an exciting, enjoyable time. As a result, the fun, excitement, and love of their courting days and honeymoon vanish.

Disagreements and Marital Problems Arise

The closer couples are brought together, the more disagreements are likely to arise to ruin the loving, honeymoon atmosphere. For

> As the day is pleasant until a storm appears,
> So is married love before cross winds blow.

When a couple first meet, they do not have anything to disagree about. Their lives have not yet become intertwined. While they are dating, they may have a few small disagreements, but that is all. When they have become engaged and are making preparations for their wedding and new life together, they begin to have some disagreements about what to do and how to do it. But when they are living together after marriage, they have a myriad of things to disagree about: a budget, domestic chores, raising the children, maintaining a home, and the list goes on endlessly.

After marriage the couple also finds out they are not adjusted to living together. They discover a number of matters they are not agreed on. Disagreements then arise between them. In addition, they may begin to experience that sometimes, living in the close confines of the same apartment or house, they get on one another's nerves. Unintentionally they irritate one another. They experience times when one of them is moody, irritable, or depressed. Consequently they experience more unpleasant times in their relationship, and they have more occasions when they are at odds with one another.

The glitter of the honeymoon further fades when they begin to see one another's unfavorable personality traits and irritating habits. They discover their mate can be selfish, possessive, lazy, or whatever. The husband becomes irritated with his wife's nylons and undergarments hanging over the shower rod. She grows increasingly irritated that he lets important matters slide until the last minute, or he leaves them for her to take care of. Such traits and personal habits strain their relationship, lead to unpleasant confrontations, and dissipate the honeymoon atmosphere they previously enjoyed.

But one thing may sap the love and affection from their relationship more than anything else: they fail to settle the disagreements and irritations that arise between them. Then they begin to feel resentment and a certain coolness come between them, and the intense love they felt during their courtship and honeymoon begins to flicker and go out.

In the above ways couples may let their hair down and fail to nurture and maintain their relationship, so that the honeymoon fades away in part or altogether. How many of the preceding honeymoon "evaporators" creep into a marriage will vary from one couple to another. The more "evaporators" that creep in, the more the honeymoon vanishes from a couple's marriage. Hopefully the preceding discussion will alert you to what to watch out for in your marriage. Certainly you do not want to look up one day, wonder what happened to your marriage, and sigh longingly for the good old days of your courtship and honeymoon when the love between you was so sweet, so pleasant, so deep.

When the Honeymoon Progresses Throughout a Marriage

Your marriage can be a growing relationship — not a fading memory. Your honeymoon should have been only the beginning of even better things to come — not the end of the good things that had been.

During each succeeding year of your marriage you can be drawn closer and bound more tightly together in an ever-deepening relationship of love and affection. That happens when both of you live and work through the hardships that arise in your life together and in your marriage itself. You are drawn closer together when both of you continue to work at making your marriage the best it can be for one another, continue to be mate-oriented, and seek to discover even more ways in which you can please each other. Your relationship deepens when both of you stay in touch with one another through intimate conversations, so you change together as you grow older and pass through the various phases of life.

If you continually work to make your relationship what the Lord made marriage, your love for one another will not grow weaker and dimmer; it will grow deeper and stronger in appreciation and understanding. When you were married, you may have enjoyed all five kinds of love in your Christian relationship. But in your youth and new marriage it was probably the delight in one another and the sexual love that especially highlighted your relationship. Now if you continue throughout your marriage to work at your relationship, not only will those two kinds of love grow more exciting and fulfilling over the years, but you will also grow to a deeper appreciation of the other kinds of love you share. Your sense of belonging to one another will increase tremendously as you both continue to experience what a refuge and source of supporting strength your mate is to you. Your friendship will become more important to both of you as you grow to understand one another through many intimate conversations over the years and as a result of the many enjoyable times you have together. Your trust in one another will grow during the years, so that both of you feel more comfortable in sharing your true inner thoughts and feelings about yourselves and the many aspects of your life and work. As Christians, by the grace of God the two of you will grow over the years in the spiritual love which can bless your marriage so richly in all that you say and do.

To cultivate a lasting honeymoon relationship, then, let us now bring together what we have learned in the earlier chapters and look at a few suggestions we have not discussed before.

By the Grace of God Be in a Right Relationship with Him

You must be in a right relationship with your Lord before you can be in a right relationship with your mate. That right relationship with your Lord comes about through repenting of your sins and trusting in Christ Jesus for forgiveness.

May the Lord, through his word and sacraments, fill both of you with appreciation for his gift of salvation. Then you both will grow spiritually in God's love for you and in your responding love for him. To honor and to serve him with a thankful love, you both will strive to conform your marriage to what he designed marriage to be. Your wills will be united with his will regarding your individual roles as husband and wife. You will also want to live according to his commandments in your marital relationship and not sin against one another. Your marital relationship will then be a blessed and happy triangular relationship such as the Lord designed for marriage.

Be Committed to Your Marriage and Mate for Life

By faith be committed to the preservation of your marriage for as long as you live. Each of you be committed to the betterment and fulfillment of your mate; neither of you concentrate on what you want from your mate. If I might be permitted to modify John F. Kennedy's words somewhat: Ask not what your mate can do for you, but what you can do for your mate.

By faith both of you be committed to fulfilling the roles of husband and wife we observed in chapter 1. Pray for God's help to fulfill them for him and for your mate. If both of you are so committed, you will be agreed on what your marriage ought to be like and what each of you needs to do to make it that way.

The more you work at your marriage, the better and happier it will be. For

Marriage is like an investment.

The more you put into it, the more you get out of it;

And if the transactions are handled wisely, it pays dividends.

Cultivate the Four Emotional Kinds of Love
in Your Marriage

Do and say the things that will continue to evoke and build those emotions in one another. Remember, your emotions are largely a response to what you perceive in each other. The more you say and do for one another, the more love you will feel for one another; the more love you feel for one another, the more you will want to do for one another. In this way your love and loving deeds for one another spiral upward in a never-ending cycle.

Communicate

Settle Your Disagreements and Conflicts the Same Day
Control Your Anger and Clear Up Your Resentment

Spend Enjoyable Time Together Having Fun and Doing Things You Both Like

Fulfill One Another Sexually

Delight in One Another

Husbands, impress your wife and make her feel like the woman she is by being that knight in shining armor for her. Honor her before one and all with the little courtesies that express how much you respect her. More than once I have heard other wives and women say admiringly, "Look! He even goes around and opens the car door for her!" If other women notice, your wife will too. She will feel like a queen because of it and make you feel like a king in return.

Dress and groom yourselves attractively for one another. Care enough to look your best. In doing so you can ignite your spouse's delight in you. An attractive-looking wife at the front door can lift her husband's flagging spirit, for example, and make him glad he came home. A little grooming and perfume or cologne when you are reunited, or before going to bed, will stimulate your senses and desire for one another.

Find impressionable ways of tenderly expressing your love for one another. Every wife is favorably impressed when occasionally she receives some flowers for no special reason other than that her husband delights in her. So if you are the husband, treat her to some flowers, or perhaps a little surprise present like a box of candy or a new dress that you select yourself. Knowing you cared enough to do it on your own lifts her spirit immensely. You show her that she does indeed please you, which is very important to her.

Would you like to fill your spouse with warm emotions and make your partner's heart glow? Then try surprising him or her with a little love note on the bedroom mirror, inside the kitchen cabinet door, or wherever your partner is sure to discover it. You might write something like, "Dearest, just a little note to let you know I love you and miss you while I am away at work. How about a date tonight?"

A pastor and friend of mine came to spend the night with us. When we saw him the next morning, he was all smiles and full of laughter. When he opened his bag that morning, he had found a large valentine from his wife of twenty-five years, expressing her love for him. Her surprise valentine is not something he will forget.

You can stimulate love and appreciation in your mate's heart with a surprise telephone call: "Hi dear! It's just your old Prince Charming with the slightly tarnished and dented armor. I simply called to tell you I love you and miss you. I can't wait to come home again to be with a real woman — you!"

Being a pastor, I have my office in my home. Periodically, from the business phone in my office I call my wife on our family's phone in another part of the house. She is always pleasantly surprised when she learns I am on the phone to tell her I love her and to ask her for a date. The warm kiss I receive a minute later when she comes into my office reveals to me the delighted love and appreciation she feels. Those telephone calls recapture for her some of the love and delight she felt more than thirty years ago before we were married. Then I used to call her long distance, from the other side of the country, while I was in the military service, to tell her that I loved her and that I wanted to marry her.

If you are a housewife, you might show your husband how much you love him by surprising him with his favorite meal or dish. There is something to be said for the old adage, "The way to a man's heart is through his stomach!"

A soft candlelight dinner alone provides a wonderful atmosphere for the two of you to delight in one another. There are times when a wife would like to be that special woman she is; times when she can dress up for her husband as she once did; times when she would enjoy going out and having her husband lavish his attention on her in a loving manner. Such a dinner can boost her feelings of self-esteem as well as her appreciation for her husband. She still needs and wants to feel that she has some of that alluring charm and beauty that captivated her husband while they were dating. The husband, on the other hand, still enjoys seeing the beautiful woman he once married and recapturing some of the magic of the good old days.

If you are unable to go out to dinner, you can still enjoy a candlelight dinner at home after the children are in bed. You can dress up for one another, get out the good dishes and the crystal wine glasses, put on some soft music, and enjoy a good meal that does not take much preparation. In the privacy of your own home you can have a delightful time together for a fraction of the price of going out.

Every husband and wife need to get away together once in a while. They married to be together and to share one another's love. That is true of you and your mate too. Such a time enables you to get away from the stress and distractions at work and at home and to relax together. You can enjoy some recreation together, a dinner and evening out, and leisurely lovemaking. Those times will reawaken the delight of being alone, the thrill of your love, the excitement of your honeymoon. I know one married couple of many years who reserved a honeymoon suite. Afterwards they said they had such a wonderful time that they will never forget it.

These are just a few of the ways you can keep the honeymoon in your marriage and deepen the love between you. And is that not what you want in your marriage? Of course it is. Otherwise, why did you read this book?

BIBLIOGRAPHY

Reference Books:

1. Ehlke, Roland Cap, *The People's Bible, Ecclesiastes, Song of Songs*, Milwaukee, Wisconsin: Northwestern Publishing House, 1988.

2. Gallatin, Judith, *Abnormal Psychology — Concepts, Issues, Trends*, New York, New York: Macmillan Publishing Co., Inc., 1982.

3. Gingrich, F. Wilbur, *Shorter Lexicon of the Greek New Testament*, Chicago and London: The University of Chicago Press, 1973.

4. Kagan, Jerome, and Havemann, Ernest, *Psychology — An Introduction*, New York, Chicago, San Francisco, Atlanta: Harcourt, Brace & World, Inc., 1968.

5. Kittel, Gerhard, editor, *Theological Dictionary of the New Testament, Volume II*, Grand Rapids, Michigan: Wm. B. Eerdmans Publishing Company, 1971.

6. Kretzmann, Paul E., *Popular Commentary of the Bible, The New Testament, Volume II*, St. Louis, Missouri: Concordia Publishing House.

7. Kuske, David P., Board for Parish Education — WELS, *Luther's Catechism*, Milwaukee, Wisconsin: Northwestern Publishing House, 1978.

8. Lenski, R.C.H., *The Interpretation of The Epistle to the Hebrews and The Epistle of James*, Minneapolis, Minnesota: Augsburg Publishing House, 1966.

9. Luther, Martin, *Commentary on the Epistle to the Romans*, translated by J. Theodore Mueller, Grand Rapids, Michigan: Kregel Publications, 1977.

10. Moulton, James Hope, and Milligan, George, *The Vocabulary of the Greek Testament*, Part III, London, New York, Toronto: Hodder and Stoughton, Limited, 1921.

11. Thayer, Joseph Henry, *Greek-English Lexicon of the New Testament*, Grand Rapids, Michigan: Zondervan Publishing House, 1975.

12. Toppe, Carleton A., *The People's Bible, 1 Corinthians*, Milwaukee, Wisconsin: Northwestern Publishing House, 1987.

13. Tregelles, Samuel Prideaux, translator of *Gesenius' Hebrew and Chaldee Lexicon to the Old Testament Scriptures*, Grand Rapids, Michigan: Wm. B. Eerdmans Publishing Company, 1971.

14. Trench, Richard C., *Synonyms of the New Testament*, Grand Rapids, Michigan: Wm. B. Eerdmans Publishing Company, 1973.

15. Webster's *New Twentieth Century Dictionary*, Unabridged, Second Edition, New York: Prentice Hall Press, 1983.

Helpful Books on Marriage:

1. Dobson, Dr. James, *What wives wish their husbands knew about women*, Wheaton, Illinois: Tyndale House Publishers, Inc., 7th printing 1981

2. Field, David, *Marriage Personalities*, Eugene, Oregon: Harvest House Publishers, 1986.

3. Gedde, Palmer, *One Plus One Equals*, Milwaukee, Wisconsin: Northwestern Publishing House, 1979.

4. Hardisty, Margaret, *Forever My Love*, Irvine, California: Harvest House Publishers, 11th printing 1978.

5. LaHaye, Tim and Beverly, *The Act of Marriage*, Grand Rapids, Michigan: Zondervan Publishing House, 1976.

6. Mace, David and Vera, *How to Have a Happy Marriage*, Nashville, Tennessee: Abingdon, 1978.

7. Osborne, Cecil, *The Art of Understanding Your Mate*, Grand Rapids, Michigan: Zondervan Publishing House, 1970.

8. Reuben, David, M.D., *Everything you always wanted to know about sex, but were afraid to ask*, New York, New York: Bantam Books, Inc., published by arrangement with David McKay Company, Inc., 36th printing, 1981.

9. Schaef, Anne Wilson, *Co-Dependence, Misunderstood — Mistreated*, San Francisco, California: Harper & Row, Publishers, 1986.

10. Swindoll, Charles R., *Strike the Original Match*, Portland, Oregon: Multnomah Press, 1980.

11. The Staff of Wisconsin Lutheran Child and Family Service, *Living In Grace*, Milwaukee, Wisconsin: 10th Anniversary Booklet, 1976.

12. Wheat, Ed, M.D., *Love Life*, Grand Rapids, Michigan: Zondervan Publishing House, 3rd printing 1981.

13. Wheat, Ed, M.D. and Gaye, *Intended for Pleasure*, Old Tappan, New Jersey: Fleming H. Revell Company, 1981 revised edition.

14. Wright, H. Norman, *Communication: Communication: Communication: Key to Your Marriage*, Ventura, California: 1984.